Praise for *GREEK MYTHOLOGY: The Gods, Goddesses, and Heroes Handbook*

"Albert gives a witty and unapologetic perspective on famous classical stories through a modern, feminist lens."

—**Rachel Smythe**, creator of the *Lore Olympus* Webtoon

"This is not your grandma's mythology primer. Liv Albert continues her work to bring Greek mythology into modern times with this refreshing, forward-thinking, and best of all, hilarious almanac. Paired with the stunning artwork by Sara Richard, the book feels like an heirloom created for our generation to pass down."

—**Emily Edwards**, author and host of the *Fuckbois of Literature* podcast

"Beautifully illustrated and instantly absorbing, *Greek Mythology: The Gods, Goddesses, and Heroes Handbook* tells the familiar stories in a fresh, entertaining way and also delves into more obscure myths, origin stories, and characters—leaving no corner of Greek mythology unexplored."

—**Jenny Williamson**, cohost of the *Ancient History Fangirl* podcast

"Gripping, deftly executed, and beautifully told, *Greek Mythology: The Gods, Goddesses, and Heroes Handbook* is at once a primer for those new to mythology and a compass for those looking to further explore the stories that still shape our world. Feminist and wise, this is a must-read for fans of *Lore Olympus* or Percy Jackson."

—**Genn McMenemy**, cohost of the *Ancient History Fangirl* podcast

Praise for GREEK MYTHOLOGY: The Gods, Goddesses, and Heroes Handbook

"I highly recommend reading this book if you want to know all the gossip straight from Mount Olympus. This will be a treasured book for any new or longtime Greek mythology obsessives."

—**Mari Phillips**, owner of MYTHSNTiTS, illustrator

"Liv brings her trademark panache to this collection! This handbook is packed with connections between ancient myth and popular culture. It's a wild ride accompanied by Sara Richard's gorgeous illustrations, suitable for those who adore mythology and enthusiastic beginners. This book is a treat for anyone who likes their ancient past with a dose of humor. We know that we do!"

—**Dr. Rad and Dr. G**, cohosts of *The Partial Historians* podcast

"Brilliant, funny, and exciting....Greek mythology can be complex, and Liv has explained it in a way that is easy to digest, with some beautiful imagery alongside the stories."

—**Jeff Murray**, artist

GREEK MYTHOLOGY

The Gods, Goddesses, and Heroes Handbook

From APHRODITE to ZEUS, a Profile of
Who's Who in Greek Mythology

LIV ALBERT

Illustrated by SARA RICHARD

Adams Media

New York   London   Toronto   Sydney   New Delhi

Adams Media
An Imprint of Simon & Schuster, Inc.
100 Technology Center Drive
Stoughton, Massachusetts 02072

First Adams Media hardcover edition March 2021

For information about special discounts for bulk purchases, please contact Simon & Schuster Special Sales at 1-866-506-1949 or business@simonandschuster.com.

The Simon & Schuster Speakers Bureau can bring authors to your live event. For more information or to book an event contact the Simon & Schuster Speakers Bureau at 1-866-248-3049 or visit our website at www.simonspeakers.com.

Interior design by Sylvia McArdle
Illustrations by Sara Richard

Manufactured in China

10 9

Library of Congress Cataloging-in-Publication Data has been applied for.

ISBN 978-1-5072-1549-4
ISBN 978-1-5072-1550-0 (ebook)

DEDICATION

For Odysseus, my first love

ACKNOWLEDGMENTS

Thank you to all of my family and friends, specifically any one of them who ever let me spout mythological facts and stories at seemingly random intervals throughout my life. Thank you to every one of the listeners of my podcast who do the same, but at much more regular intervals. Thank you to my pandemic friends, Genn and Jenny (of the *Ancient History Fangirl* podcast!), who cheered me on while I wrote this book....I needed it.

CONTENTS

INTRODUCTION

Escaping a labyrinth after killing the vicious monster that lives in it…lusting after your own reflection…hunting with a female warrior who's a whiz with a bow and arrow: The world of Greek mythology is filled with danger, love, adventure—and lots of family dysfunction. There's a good reason the stories are still being told today in books, movies, TV shows, and webcomics: Greek myths are eternal and endlessly entertaining. Gods, goddesses, creatures great and small, and mere mortals join together in dramatic, fascinating, hilarious, and often violent tales of nature and humanity's flaws and foibles.

Though they often had otherworldly powers, ancient Greek gods and goddesses were very…human. They got jealous and angry; they were vengeful and manipulative; they were always making mistakes and doing things they were told not to do. This endless parade of remarkable characters and their tales can be confusing and hard to remember, so let *Greek Mythology: The Gods, Goddesses, and Heroes Handbook* tell you dozens of their stories in a clear, engaging way.

This book is broken down into four parts:

1. **What Is Greek Mythology?:** a beginner section that outlines what you need to know to get started (how and when did these stories originate, anyway?)
2. **The Olympians:** character profiles for all the Olympian gods
3. **Deities, Etc.:** these are the characters who aren't Olympians but aren't mortal either
4. **Heroes and Mortals:** the major heroic and mortal players of Greek mythology

Each key character gets their own entry, in which you can learn their name and aliases; what place, topic, or trade they ruled; their origin story; and the most famous adventure they're involved in. Some character entries include subcharacters: gods or mortals so closely associated with that character that they are best learned about together.

Whether you want to brush up on your trivia (which god is the dwarf planet Pluto named after?), better understand a piece of pop culture (such as Rachel Smythe's Webtoon *Lore Olympus* or everyone's favorite Disney animated film, *Hercules*), or just enjoy these exciting stories, *Greek Mythology: The Gods, Goddesses, and Heroes Handbook* gives you a front-row seat for the outrageous trials and tribulations of these ancient superstars.

PART 1

WHAT IS GREEK MYTHOLOGY?

Greek mythology began as an oral tradition thousands of years ago. The ancient Greeks used these stories to understand and explain the natural world around them. How was the world created? Where did humanity begin? Over time these myths were passed down; eventually some were written down as epic poems or, later, as plays that were performed in front of audiences of thousands of spectators in the world's first theaters.

The stories of the ancient Greeks revolved almost exclusively around the characters in them. Their stories are universal and very much resemble the stories and themes told today in books and movies and on television—good versus evil, triumph over adversity, rooting for the underdog, and so on. Greek mythology and its characters have inspired, and are still inspiring, new works of popular culture. The stories are eternal, universal, and truly some of the most thrilling and entertaining works of fiction. But, of course, the ancient

Greeks (for the most part) believed their stories were not fiction at all but rather history or, sometimes, contemporary anecdotes of encounters with gods and monsters. What makes Greek mythology so special is the way the gods interacted with the humans in creative, manipulative, and often violent ways. A warning: The gods assaulted other gods, nymphs, and mortals often.

———◆———

An important note about Greek mythology in general is, in a word, variation. Because the stories were told orally over hundreds, sometimes thousands, of years, there are many different versions and interpretations. In order to properly tell these stories, certain variations have been selected for this book so as not to confuse you with endless asides of "According to..." and "But another source...," although some alternate sources have been included.

The Romans also took many Greek gods and myths and made them their own. While they were often portrayed differently in the respective cultures, they had shared origins. Because of this, the two cultures' mythologies are often conflated. There are some select Roman stories referenced here (the Roman poet Ovid was a really good storyteller), but it's always made clear when the story being told is of Roman origin.

———◆———

The Creation Myth: Gods and Titans

The world of Greek mythology began with Chaos, a mass of nothingness from which sprang Gaia. Also known as Mother Earth, Gaia was the personification of the earth itself. She quickly became lonely and created herself a husband, Ouranos (yes, like Uranus, the planet). Together they spawned:

1. **The Titans**, a group very similar to the gods, humanlike and different mostly only in name and overall importance in the mythology; they are sometimes also referred to as gods.
2. **The Hecatonchires**, a very cool, if rarely mentioned, race of monsters, each with one hundred hands and fifty heads.

One of the Titans, Kronos, became power hungry and obsessed with overthrowing those above him in the hierarchy of deities. Kronos castrated his father, Ouranos, and threw the body parts he'd removed from his father into the sea. From the falling droplets of blood were born two types of creatures:

1. **The Erinyes**, better known as the Furies, three women whose lives were devoted to punishing those who broke the natural laws of the world.
2. **The Gigantes**, a race of bloodthirsty giants.

So, Kronos had made a name for himself...but it wasn't a good one. His mother, Gaia, was then hell-bent on overthrowing him and regaining her own power. And even Kronos's wife, Rhea, another Titan, quickly tired of him. Not because she was angry about what he did to Ouranos (also her father; there were a lot of shared parents among couples in Greek mythology—it's best not to think too hard about it) but because every time she gave birth to one of their children, Kronos simply ate the child whole. There was a prophecy that a child of Kronos would one day overthrow him just as he did his own father, and Kronos believed he could nip it in the bud by eating the children.

Rhea gave birth to five children, all of whom Kronos ate before they could utter a sound. Finally, fed up (rightfully so!) with all her children being eaten, Rhea arranged to have her next child whisked away before Kronos could see him and brought down to earth to Mount Ida, on the island of Crete. There the child would be raised far away from his father and, with any luck, would live to adulthood and be able to fulfill the prophecy that Kronos feared. When Rhea gave birth to her sixth child, he was whisked away as planned. In place of the baby, Rhea handed Kronos a large rock swaddled like a newborn, which he swallowed. The child, meanwhile, was brought to Crete and named Zeus.

In time, Zeus grew up to become the strong, powerful god who his father had always feared. As with nearly all prophecies in Greek mythology, the one feared by Kronos came true. Zeus, with the help of his mother, snuck up on Kronos and forced him to vomit up his children, Zeus's siblings. One by one, Poseidon, Hades, Hera, Demeter, and Hestia were "reborn" from Kronos's stomach. These children of the Titans overthrew and imprisoned Kronos and the Titans who sided with him in a war known as the Titanomachy. The children then positioned themselves on Mount Olympus, the new home to the gods, and gave themselves the name Olympians from it.

Eventually these original Olympians coupled up with each other and with other deities (stories of these couplings are told in their character entries), and with that, the Olympians were complete (sort of...details on that to come). They were Zeus, Poseidon, Hades, Demeter, Hera, Athena, Aphrodite, Apollo, Artemis, Hephaestus, Ares, Hermes, Dionysus, and Hestia.

There were technically only ever twelve Olympians at a time.
Hestia eventually gave up her spot to Dionysus (she was never all
that into their drama), and Demeter wasn't always considered to
be one, but as one of the original siblings, she deserves
her place in the story (more on that later).

The Olympians went on to create the natural world on earth, including creating humans themselves (that story is told in the entries on Prometheus and Pandora). Once they had created that world, they decided to wreak havoc on it and its people any time the desire arose (and it arose often).

Gods, Heroes, Mortals, and Monsters

The Olympians were the most powerful of the Greek gods, but there were hundreds of other gods and deities in the mythology. The word *deities* is used broadly here: They were humanlike characters who were (for our purposes) not Olympians but also not mortals. There are a lot of characters in Greek mythology that fall under this category.

There were the Titans who weren't imprisoned with Kronos, like Prometheus and Epimetheus, as well as other gods both major and minor that have important stories to be told, like Eros (Cupid). There were heroes, some the children of gods and others pure mortals with epic and famous histories (like Heracles, Perseus, Cadmus, and more!). Their stories are equally important and equally dramatic even when they don't include encounters with the Olympians…though they usually do, in one way or another.

You'll also encounter everyday humans who also figured into many stories of Greek mythology. These mortals were often used as the playthings of gods, as mothers of heroes by those gods, or as examples of hubris to be punished by the gods (Tantalus, anyone?).

And then there are the monsters. The nonhuman creatures and monsters of Greek mythology are some of the most memorable: Who hasn't heard of the Cyclopes or the many-headed Hydra? Many of the most famous and murderous monsters of Greek mythology were the children of Typhon and Echidna, who were two of the original monsters (more on those two in their entry).

Other Important Deities

⬳ Nymphs were minor deities associated with different aspects of nature. There were a great many types of nymphs, grouped by where they lived and what they were devoted to. The most common types of nymphs were:

- **Naiads** were nymphs of rivers, streams, and other bodies of fresh water. A subset of these were called Oceanids, freshwater nymphs who were specifically daughters of the Titan Oceanus, the personification of the great river that the Greeks believed encircled the world (yes, it's confusing that Oceanids were *freshwater* nymphs).
- **Dryads** and **Hamadryads** were nymphs of the forests; their job was to protect the trees of the woods. Hamadryads differ from Dryads in that these nymphs were each devoted to a specific tree.
- **Hesperides** were nymphs of the sunset, daughters of the Titan Hesperis, the evening star. They guarded the Garden of the Hesperides, where famed golden apples grew.

- **Nereids** were nymphs of the sea and typically daughters of various sea gods and Titans, including Nereus.
- **Lampades** were the nymphs of the Underworld. They carried torches through the world of the dead and accompanied the goddesses Persephone and Hecate.

◈ The nine Muses (*Mousai* in Greek; *Musae* in Latin) were goddesses of knowledge, music, and dance and were the inspiration for all artists, poets, and playwrights of ancient Greece. They were the daughters of Zeus and the Titan Mnemosyne, the goddess of memory. Each muse was goddess of a specific aspect of inspiration: Calliope was the muse of epic poetry, Thalia of comedy, Euterpe of lyric poetry, Terpsichore of dance and choral song, Melpomene of tragedy, Polyhymnia of religious hymns, Erato of erotic poetry, Clio of history, and Ourania of astronomy.

◈ The Fates, or the Moirae (their original Greek name), were the three goddesses who determined the fate of every individual on earth. The ancient Greeks believed a person's fate was woven into a thread of life, all handled by the Fates. The goddess Clotho spun a person's life thread, creating their life; the goddess Lachesis measured the person's life thread, determining their life span; and the goddess Atropos handled the cutting of a person's life thread and therefore their death. You may recognize this concept from the 1997 Disney film *Hercules*. In that version, the Fates are conflated with another trio of women from Greek mythology, the Graeae, three crones who shared one eye and one tooth between them.

◈ The Furies, or the Erinyes (their original Greek name), as briefly mentioned earlier, were goddesses of vengeance and retribution. These goddesses were in charge of punishing humans for their crimes, particularly murder of family members. Their names were Alecto, Megaera, and Tisiphone, and they were depicted as monstrous, with wings, and snakes for hair or snakes coiled around their limbs.

One of the torturous professors in *Harry Potter and the Deathly Hallows*, Alecto Carrow, was named for one of the Furies. The name of Alecto's brother, Amycus, also came from Greek mythology: Amycus was a man who killed people by imprisoning them in a box.

← Sirens were monsters that were half women, half birds. They were both monstrous and beautiful, and were best known for their song, which they would use to lure sailors out of their boats and to their deaths. The only way to safely pass by the Sirens was to completely block your ears with wax so not a single note of their song could get through. Odysseus famously wanted to hear the Sirens' song, so he tied himself to the mast of his ship so he could hear it without jumping in the water (the men on his ship used wax, so they were not affected).

← Satyrs and centaurs were the most famous half-human creatures. Satyrs were top-half human, bottom-half goat, and were typically found causing trouble (both lighthearted and not!). Centaurs, meanwhile, were top-half human, bottom-half horse and, with the exception of Chiron (he trained many of the heroes and was the inspiration for the satyr named Phil in the 1997 animated film *Hercules*!), were horrible creatures.

PART 2

THE OLYMPIANS

The ancient Greek pantheon of gods is extensive. There is a god or minor deity for almost everything you can imagine. Dawn and dusk? There are gods for that. Epic poetry? There's a muse for that. Even individual rivers and streams were likely to have a god devoted to them. But the gods who *really* mattered were the Olympians: the original gods, the ones who defeated the Titans and created the world as we know it. Zeus assigned the other Olympians tasks to create the plants, the animals, and even the humans of earth.

The Olympians believed that because they *created* the creatures and people of earth, they also had every right to *mess with* those same people. And so they did—the Olympians caused endless problems for the humans of earth. Sometimes they brought storms and plagues upon them; other times they would fall "in love" with the people of earth. It was never *real* love, though; it was a desire for power and control. The Olympians wanted *a lot* of power.

There were always twelve Olympians, but those twelve varied depending on the time period and the source. They were made up of the original siblings: Zeus, Poseidon, and Hera, and sometimes Hades, Demeter, and/or Hestia. Demeter isn't always considered an Olympian—sometimes she is one and Hades is not; other times, it's the other way around. Later, as the mythology and stories of the gods evolved, Hestia, too, left her seat at the table of the Olympian gods. From there, children of the original siblings joined the group: Athena, the twins Apollo and Artemis, and Hermes (all children of Zeus); Hephaestus, child of Hera; Ares, child of Zeus and Hera; Aphrodite, sometimes daughter of Zeus, sometimes daughter of Ouranos (you can read all about it in Aphrodite's entry); and Dionysus, the last Olympian to join the fray, replacing Hestia. Dionysus was unique because he was the son of Zeus and a mortal woman.

ZEUS

God of the Sky, Weather, Destiny, and Law and Order; King of the Gods

AKA: Jupiter; Jove (both Roman/Latin)

᠌᠌᠌᠌᠌᠌

What's His Deal?

Zeus was the king of the gods. Technically, he was the god of the sky, the weather, and the like, but *really* he was the god of all gods; the god who got his way *every time*; the god who used his power and influence to ruin nearly everyone he came into contact with. Though he appears in almost every pop culture representation of Greek mythology, Zeus was far from the loving, doting father of Disney's *Hercules* and a bit more like Liam Neeson's Zeus in the 2010 film *Clash of the Titans*. Zeus spent his time pitting gods against one another and descending upon any and all women (and sometimes men) he came across (human, nymph, goddess, you name it!) to "seduce" them or "carry them off." These terms, among others, are euphemisms for what Zeus really did: assaulted them. Zeus was incredibly predatory—there are *countless* examples of him preying upon unsuspecting gods and mortals.

You'll find specific examples of Zeus's more troubling "escapades" with women, nymphs, and goddesses in the entries on Leto, Semele, Io, Europa, and Leda (and there are *so many* more that couldn't be included here).

Zeus was best known for his thunderbolts, the weapons he would use against enemies, which symbolized his control of the sky and weather. Eagles were also believed to be symbols of Zeus in the ancient world, often seen as omens (in the *Iliad*, the story of the Trojan War, an eagle holding a snake in its talons was seen as a message from Zeus). Finally, the bull, while not always an explicit symbol of Zeus, was often associated with him because of his choice to appear in the form of a bull (see the entry on Europa).

The Story You Need to Know

When it comes to Zeus, the stories are endless; in fact, he features in most of the stories you'll read here. Zeus's real claim to fame, though, was the sheer volume of children he had, how he fathered them, and who they were.

＊ He fathered the nine Muses with the Titan Mnemosyne; with the Titan Themis, Zeus fathered the Horae, who were the goddesses of the seasons, and the Moirae (the Fates); with the Titan Eurynome, Zeus fathered the Charities, the goddesses of grace and beauty; and Zeus was the father of Persephone with his sister, Demeter.

- Through Zeus's marriage to his sister (try to ignore how weird that is) Hera, he was the father of the god of war, Ares; the goddess of youth, Hebe; and the goddess of childbirth, Eileithyia.

- After Zeus's marriage to Hera, he fathered the twins Apollo and Artemis with the Titan Leto.

- With the Titan Metis he was the father of the goddess Athena.

- With the nymph Maia he was the father of the god Hermes.

- Finally, through an encounter with the mortal woman Semele, Zeus was the father of the god Dionysus.

And that's just the more notable god children (there are so, *so* many more)!

The king of the gods was also the father of some of the most well-known mortals of Greek mythology. The hero Heracles was Zeus's son by a woman named Alcmene; the hero Perseus was Zeus's son by a woman named Danaë. The famous king of Crete, Minos, the reason the ancient Cretan culture are known as the Minoans, was Zeus's son by a woman named Europa. The famed Helen of Sparta (and later, Troy) and her infamous sister Clytemnestra were (sort of, but we'll get to that) Zeus's daughters by a woman named Leda.

This isn't a comprehensive list of Zeus's children, just a taste of the most famous of them. The king of the gods was also known as the father of the gods, for both literal and figurative reasons. While most gods you'll read about here have distinct stories associated with them directly, Zeus's stories involve so many gods and mortals that those stories are told in each of their individual entries.

Now You Know

Most of the moons of the planet Jupiter have been named after "lovers" of Zeus (again, he was really more of an *assaulter*): Europa, Io, and Callisto, to name a few. Interestingly, the NASA spacecraft *Juno* orbits Jupiter. Basically, this means NASA sent Zeus's wife to watch over him and the women he had affairs with.

POSEIDON

God of the Sea, Horses, and Earthquakes

AKA: Neptune (Roman/Latin); Earth-Shaker

〜〜〜〜〜〜〜〜

What's His Deal?

Poseidon was one of the original Olympians, a brother of Zeus, and, famously, the god of the sea. Poseidon was also the god of horses, which likely came from the belief that waves can look like galloping horses. The ancient Greeks believed that Poseidon gave them earthquakes, so they gave him the epithet (which is sort of a nickname but is often used in conjunction with the person's name) *Earth-shaker*. Both horses and dolphins were symbolic of Poseidon, and he was often shown in art riding a chariot pulled by a *hippocamp*, a creature that was half horse and half fish.

Poseidon was married to the nymph Amphitrite, and they had a number of children; the most notable was Triton. This son of Poseidon is the origin of Ariel's father's name in the 1989 animated film *The Little Mermaid*. The film version of that king of Atlantica, however, is based more on Poseidon himself than his son. Like Poseidon, the Triton of *The Little Mermaid* carried a

trident. Unlike the film character Triton, Poseidon wasn't known for being particularly nice or loving. Instead, he was famous for being...difficult, and for the punishments he doled out on unsuspecting heroes and mortals. Like his brother Zeus, Poseidon also had a tendency to assault women and nymphs. Poseidon was also the father of Percy (Perseus) in the Percy Jackson series (though, mythologically, Perseus was the son of Zeus, whereas Theseus was often described as the son of Poseidon).

The Story You Need to Know

Before the ancient city-state of Athens was named Athens, the people of the city held a competition for which god would be the city's patron, and therefore which god the city would be named after. Both the goddess Athena and the god Poseidon put their names into the ring. In order to prove their worth to the city, each god offered up the best thing they could think of to bestow upon the unnamed city, then the people would choose their favorite. It was a pretty good deal for the humans: Either way, they would get something valuable for their new city.

The competition was held on what would become the Acropolis hill at the center of the city. There, the gods made their offerings: Poseidon struck the ground on the hill with his trident and a stream of water erupted, gushing from the earth. Poseidon was offering the people a constant supply of water—a worthy proposal that was clearly something a burgeoning city could use (according to other sources, Poseidon also gave Athens its first horse). Athena caused an olive tree to grow from the ground before the gathered crowd. The olive tree, she told the people, could provide them not only with wood but also with fruit that could be eaten and from which they could make oil. The people selected Athena's offering and named their city after the goddess.

After his defeat in Athens, Poseidon continued trying to become the patron of various cities in Greece and had a habit of fighting the other gods for this honor. In the city of Troezen, he once again fought Athena for the title, but in that case Zeus decided they would both get to be the city's patrons. Poseidon fought with Hera over the city of Argos (she won), and he fought with the Titan Helios over the city of Corinth (Poseidon actually won that one!).

Now You Know

According to mythology, it was Poseidon (along with Apollo) who built the walls around the famous city of Troy but later sent a sea monster to attack the city when its king didn't properly thank him for the walls! The hero Heracles eventually killed the sea monster and saved the city of Troy, but Poseidon never gave up his grudge.

HADES

God of the Underworld and Wealth; God and King of the Dead

AKA: Aidoneus; Plouton/Pluto (Greek and Roman/Latin name); Dis (Roman/Latin)

▱▱▱▱▱

What's His Deal?

Like his brothers, Zeus and Poseidon, Hades was one of the original Olympian gods, a son of the Titans Kronos and Rhea. You might know him as the fiery-haired villain in Disney's *Hercules* or the hunky love interest of Rachel Smythe's *Lore Olympus* (two *very* different interpretations of the god!). Hades was the god of the dead and the Underworld, but he was *not* the god of death (that was a guy named Thanatos). He was also the god of wealth and riches. *Dis*, one of his Latin names, means "rich." Hades had a helmet of invisibility that was made by the Cyclopes during the war between the gods and the Titans (it sounds cool, but it doesn't really come up in the mythology very much).

Many of the Roman/Latin names of the gods are also the names of the planets in our solar system. But, unlike most of the others, Pluto is not just his Roman name; it is also Greek! Hades was called Pluto (or Plouton) in certain cult worship situations and, later, even more broadly, including in some Greek plays.

Hades was married to Persephone, his niece, whom he kidnapped as a girl (*awkward*). The origins of their story are tragic and awful, though things do somehow end up marginally well for all parties (a real feat in Greek mythology). Even though he was the god of the dead and is often featured as the villain in popular culture, beyond his kidnapping of Persephone, Hades was actually one of the least troubling of the Olympian gods. Hades was faithful to his wife, and they seemed to have grown to love, or at least respect, each other and lived quite contentedly in the Underworld. Otherwise, he mostly kept to himself, keeping track of those who died and causing little to no trouble among other gods or the living mortals. His brother Zeus was far more dangerous, yet it's usually poor Hades who's depicted as the villain.

Now You Know

While "Hades" was the god of the Underworld's *name*, that name can also refer to the Underworld itself: as in "Heracles traveled to Hades to steal a dog" (see the upcoming entry on Cerberus for that crazy quest!). The Underworld is also referred to as Tartarus, though this word could refer to both a specific part of the Underworld or the place as a whole. It's most often used to describe the place where all the eternal punishments took place.

Persephone

Goddess of Vegetation, Spring, and the Underworld

AKA: Kore; Proserpine (Roman/Latin)

Persephone was the daughter of Demeter and Zeus and was originally the goddess of spring and growth. Persephone's two Greek names, *Kore* and *Persephone*, were used before Hades kidnapped her and after, respectively. First, her name was Kore, meaning "young girl" or "maiden" (as in "virgin"). After the kidnapping, she took the name Persephone, which means "to destroy" or "to bring death" (way cooler), since she had become an infernal goddess of death and queen of the Underworld. Even though her initial arrival in the Underworld was tragic and *problematic* (see the upcoming story), Persephone made the place her own, becoming the true queen of the Underworld. While simultaneously remaining the goddess of spring, Persephone took on this role of infernal goddess of death wholeheartedly, becoming known as the Dread Goddess, and often being more respected and feared than her husband, the original god of the dead.

The kidnapping of Persephone is typically referred to as the "rape of Persephone." *Rape* was used interchangeably with *kidnap* in this context, but it was also connected to the idea of taking women as property and therefore having full rights over them and their bodies. It meant "kidnap" and, by extension, "sexual assault."

Persephone spent part of the year with her mother, Demeter, on earth, and the rest in the Underworld with her husband. When Persephone was with Demeter, the earth thrived and all the plants grew. When she was with her husband, the crops withered and were covered over by frost. She therefore became associated both with spring and growth and with the process of the earth retreating into itself in hibernation over the winter months.

While Persephone and Hades didn't have any children (though some sources say they were the parents of the Furies), Persephone did have children by her father, Zeus (...*yeah*).

The Story You Need to Know

Hades first appeared before Persephone in a field. She had been picking flowers peacefully with her friends, the Oceanids, but strayed away from them and was left alone, distracted by the beautiful narcissus before her. Suddenly, the earth opened before her and there was Hades, god of the dead and king of the Underworld. He grabbed Persephone, dragging her forcefully into his chariot pulled by coal-black horses. In an instant, they were back beneath the earth, traveling to the Underworld. The cry she uttered when Hades grabbed her was brief and reached only the goddess Hecate, who told Persephone's mother, Demeter, what she had heard (the entry on Demeter will cover her side of the story). Hades felt he had the right to appear before Persephone and take her by force because her father, Zeus, had given him permission directly. Both Zeus and Hades knew that Demeter would never allow it if she were asked, so they didn't.

Demeter raged upon the earth in search of her daughter and brought the whole of it to a standstill. Finally, she was able to convince Zeus to force Hades to relinquish Persephone. Through this order of Zeus, Persephone may have been able to leave the Underworld for good—but she had eaten some pomegranate seeds that Hades had given her. Having eaten this food of the Underworld, Persephone would have to spend one-third of her time there with her new husband, Hades (the kidnapping had automatically resulted in their marriage). She would then be able to spend the remaining two-thirds of the year with the other gods on Olympus, and with her mother, Demeter. This duality of Persephone's position in the world, both above- and belowground, was, the ancient Greeks believed, why the seasons of the harvest existed.

This story of the relationship of Hades and Persephone is often retold more romantically than it originally appeared in the mythology, and in recent years it has become one of the most popular myths. Most notably, Rachel Smythe's Webtoon *Lore Olympus* retells the story of Hades and Persephone, and Persephone's transition from the maiden Kore into the Dread Goddess of the Underworld, Persephone, in a beautifully modern world.

Hecate

Goddess of Magic, Witchcraft, Ghosts, and Necromancy

———◆———

Hecate is one of the most mysterious characters of Greek mythology. She was likely the daughter of the Titans Perses and Asteria and was typically shown in Greek art holding torches. Due to this, and the mystery around her in general, she was either considered a Titan herself or a minor goddess, but in either case she was a fascinating, important, and very powerful *witch*. Hecate practiced what the ancient Greeks called *pharmaka*, which was the use of herbs and plants to create potions and the like (where we get the word *pharmac*y). Hecate was believed to have discovered a number of poisonous plants and potions that she would use to tip javelins and spears, making them far more deadly. According to some sources, Hecate would also test these poisons and potions on strangers she came across: She'd feed strangers poisoned food and watch to see how they reacted.

Hecate was best known for guiding the goddess Demeter (with those aforementioned torches) as the goddess searched for her kidnapped daughter, Persephone. It was Hecate who heard Persephone cry out, though she didn't immediately know who had taken her. Once Persephone was located living in the Underworld with Hades, Hecate became her companion in the world of the dead.

The witch goddess was said to spend her time at crossroads or tombs and was often accompanied by a polecat and a dog, who was originally a woman named Hecuba, the queen of Troy. Hecuba refused to go as a slave with the Greeks after the fall of Troy—instead, she jumped into the sea and was transformed into a dog.

According to some, in her role as infernal goddess alongside Persephone, Hecate often spent her time wandering with the souls of the dead, her presence announced by the ominous howling of dogs.

Like a number of other goddesses of Greek mythology (like Hestia, for example), Hecate was incredibly important in the Greek world, but there are very few, if any, recorded stories about her.

Cerberus

Guardian of the Underworld

Cerberus was Hades's loyal guardian of the Underworld. One of the most famous "monsters" of Greek mythology, Cerberus was an enormous three-headed dog that both guarded the Underworld against unwanted intruders and kept the souls of the dead safely within its boundaries. While he is most well known for being simply a three-headed dog, Cerberus is sometimes described as having a snake for a tail in addition to a mane of snakes. According to some, his slobber was poisonous and may have been used by the witch Hecate. Cerberus was a child of the original monsters Typhon and Echidna and thereby sibling to many of the other most impressive and famous monsters of mythology.

In popular culture, a version of Cerberus appears in the first Harry Potter book as Hagrid's dog, Fluffy, positioned to guard the location of the sorcerer's stone. In Greek mythology, he was most famous for being captured by the hero Heracles as the last of his Twelve Labors. (Cerberus features briefly in Disney's *Hercules* in that same role, though he isn't given much screen time.)

In that story, a man named Eurystheus assigned the labor to Heracles: Travel to the Underworld, capture and bring back the vicious Hound of Hades, Cerberus. Eurystheus intended for this to kill Heracles; he didn't actually want to see the monstrous dog. According to some, Heracles completed the labor with the help of Persephone—she gave Heracles the dog, and he brought him back to Eurystheus without incident. According to others, Hades instructed Heracles that he could take the dog, provided he was able to overcome the beast without weapons…he could use only his own two hands. Heracles was the strongest of all the Greek heroes, and he was able to take down Cerberus and bring him back to Eurystheus with no trouble at all.

The famous musician and hero Orpheus also encountered Cerberus on his journey to the Underworld to bring back his wife, Eurydice. As with Fluffy in Harry Potter, Orpheus was able to lull the monstrous dog into a calm sleep by playing music.

DEMETER

Goddess of Agriculture and the Harvest

AKA: Ceres (Roman/Latin)

⊑⊇⊑⊇⊑⊇⊑⊇

What's Her Deal?

Demeter was one of the firstborn gods (daughter of Kronos and Rhea) and is most famous for being the mother of Persephone, queen of the Underworld. As the goddess of agriculture and the harvest, she controlled the farming of the ancient Greeks and was vital to their day-to-day life.

Demeter also became the presiding goddess of the Eleusinian Mysteries, secret rituals of a "mystery cult" whose initiates were understood to find themselves in a special place in the Underworld upon their deaths: the blessed Elysium. These weren't like modern cults; they were simply groups of people whose worship and practices were kept secret to all but those officially initiated. The Eleusinian Mysteries were the most important of all ancient Greek mystery cults.

The Story You Need to Know

When Demeter's daughter, Persephone, was kidnapped by Hades, Demeter panicked. At first, she had no idea what had happened to her daughter. For nine days, Demeter searched the earth day and night for her daughter, and in that time she didn't eat or drink anything at all. Finally, she met with the witch goddess Hecate, who told her she had heard Persephone cry out when she'd been taken but hadn't seen who'd done it. She offered to help Demeter continue her search. Together they went to see the Titan Helios—as the god who brought the sun across the sky each day, he would have seen Persephone being taken. It was Helios who told Demeter that Hades, the god of the Underworld, had kidnapped her daughter. Helios also told Demeter that it had been done with the consent of Zeus.

This information—that her brother, Persephone's own father (…*yeah*) had given Hades permission to *kidnap* her—was the final straw for Demeter. Her panic and fear turned to rage, and she was determined not to return to Olympus. Instead, she wandered the earth in absolute fury and despair. Because she was the goddess of agriculture, her despair affected the earth itself. Nothing grew while Demeter was in this state: Crops withered and died, and the earth grew dry and barren.

Eventually, Demeter's searching brought her to the city of Eleusis, where she disguised herself as a mortal woman in order to visit with the king and his family. At this point she was just searching for something to give her meaning and distract her from how much she missed her daughter. She became the nurse to the family's new baby, Demophoön. Demeter grew to love the child so much that she couldn't bear the idea that he could ever die, so she decided to make him immortal. In order to do this, she placed him in the embers of the fire overnight. One night, Demophoön's mother witnessed what Demeter was doing and screamed in horror (what a terrifying thing to see!). Demeter was angry with her—she had only been trying to help the baby! She revealed herself as the goddess and reprimanded the baby's mother. Demeter then left Eleusis in anger, and the people built a temple in an attempt to appease her.

Eventually the barren earth caused by Demeter's despair became too much, and Zeus knew he needed to do something about the situation. He begged and pleaded with Demeter to bring life back to the earth, but she wouldn't until she was certain she would have her daughter back. Eventually Zeus relented and forced Hades to return Persephone, but before he did, Hades fed her a few pomegranate seeds. Having eaten fruit of the Underworld, Persephone was forced to split her time between her mother and her new husband. This annual tradition is how the ancient Greeks understood the transition between seasons and the barrenness of the earth during the winter, when Persephone was in the Underworld with her husband and her mother despaired, missing her daughter.

Now You Know

The gods had some very strange ways of making mortals immortal or invulnerable. Demeter placed Demophoön in the embers of a roaring fire, and Thetis, Achilles's goddess mother, dipped him in a cauldron. Both women were caught by nosy mortals who didn't understand what they were doing, and the procedures were interrupted (Peleus, Achilles's father, caught Thetis in the act), thereby affecting the fates of the children.

HERA

Goddess of Marriage, Women, and Fertility; Queen of the Gods

AKA: Juno (Roman/Latin)

᠎᠎᠎᠎᠎᠎

What's Her Deal?

Hera was, somewhat ironically, the goddess of marriage and the wife of Zeus (though Zeus was not particularly respectful of marital vows, she was). She was the goddess of marriage, but she was also the goddess who frequently punished women for her husband's desire to have sex with, or assault, them. Hera rarely punished Zeus himself, which could have been because it was so much harder to punish the king of the gods than it was mortal women, or because she actually blamed the women. Regardless, Hera's role in most stories involves her attempts to ruin women or their children by Zeus. You probably know Hera from Disney's *Hercules*, a version of her that is lovely but very different from the original myth.

Hera's role in Disney's *Hercules* is much more entertaining when you know the truth about her marriage with Zeus, let alone her relationship with Heracles! Most of Heracles's life was spent trying to avoid the deadly obstacles presented to him by Hera.

Most of Zeus's many, many children were born of other women, but his own wife was the mother of at least three of his children: Ares, the god of war and their only Olympian child; Hebe, the goddess of youth (who eventually married Heracles); and Eileithyia, the goddess of childbirth. But Hera had another child, Hephaestus, whom she bore *without* the help of Zeus, or any man at all! Hera was so angry with her husband for constantly cheating on her with other women (both with and without their consent), and she was even angrier because those women were constantly bearing him children (both gods and mortals). She was most angry with Athena, whom she saw as being born of Zeus alone (Athena did have a mother, but Zeus had eaten her!—see Athena's entry), and so Hera impregnated herself with the god Hephaestus (his entry tells the full story) so she could have a child who was all her own.

The Story You Need to Know

Hera plays a small role in many stories of Greek mythology, typically as she punishes her husband's many, *many* indiscretions. One of the more interesting stories featuring Hera involves a man named Ixion, who found himself quite taken with her. He believed that he "loved her," but in truth the man had simply decided he wouldn't rest until he found the goddess and had sex with her, whether or not she wanted to. So, Ixion found Hera and tried to assault her. Hera was able to fend him off and immediately went to tell Zeus what had happened. Zeus was furious when he heard what Ixion had done and decided he would tempt Ixion again, in order to catch him in the act. Thankfully, he knew better than to use the real Hera as bait. Instead, Zeus transformed a cloud so that it looked and acted like Hera and then placed the cloud within reach of Ixion. Of course, Ixion was fooled by this cloud and at once assaulted the woman he believed was Hera. When Ixion later bragged about what he'd done, Zeus, furious, found him and carried out one of the more creative punishments doled out on mortals: Ixion was strapped to a fiery wheel that rolled through the sky (or, some say, the Underworld) for eternity.

Meanwhile the cloud-Hera (named Nephele) became pregnant when she was assaulted by Ixion, eventually giving birth, *via raindrops* on Mount Pelion, to the race of centaurs (half human, half horse).

Now You Know

Hera was so affected by the death of her beloved guardian, Argus Panoptes, at the hands of Hermes (see Io's entry for this story) that she memorialized the hundred-eyed giant by placing each of his eyes in the feathers of the peacock and taking on the bird as her symbolic animal. This, the ancient Greeks theorized, is why the feathers of peacocks look like eyes.

ATHENA

Goddess of Strategic War and Wisdom

AKA: Pallas Athene; Minerva (Roman/Latin)

᠎᠎᠎᠎᠎᠎᠎

What's Her Deal?

Athena was Zeus's favorite daughter, and he made this distinction very clear throughout his life. She was the daughter of the king of the gods and the Titan Metis. Some say that Metis was Zeus's first wife; others say she was his first affair. In either case, when Zeus and Metis were together, Metis became pregnant with the goddess Athena. But shortly after this, Zeus learned that any child of Metis was destined to be much wiser than himself. Zeus was immediately threatened by this prospect and sought to stop any child of Metis from ever existing. His solution to this "problem" was to swallow Metis whole.

After Metis was swallowed, however, her pregnancy continued from within Zeus's stomach. Eventually Zeus began to feel the effects of Metis's growing fetus inside. He found himself with a horrible headache, the pain of which he simply couldn't manage. He consulted others on Mount Olympus about how he should handle what he was experiencing. It was suggested that Zeus cleave at his own head with an axe, because surely that would relieve the pressure and clear up his horrible migraine. Zeus agreed to this suggestion and asked the god Hephaestus to be the one who aimed the axe. Hephaestus did, and from the newly made hole in Zeus's head his daughter Athena sprang, fully grown and clad in armor, brandishing her shield.

Athena is one of the most famous gods. She was the patron goddess of many prominent ancient cities, including, of course, Athens. Her Roman name, Minerva, was used as the first name of Professor McGonagall in the Harry Potter series, probably to signify McGonagall's wisdom and bravery.

The Story You Need to Know

Athena had a part in the successes of most of the heroes of ancient Greece—she was always there to help in whatever way she could. With a heavy hand, Athena influenced the Greek side of the Trojan War. (She and Hera teamed up to help the Greeks beat the Trojans whenever they could.)

When it came to later myths, though, she sometimes played a different role (see the entry on Medusa). For example, in myths retold by the Roman poet Ovid, Athena is often a punisher of women.

This story is one of those examples. Arachne was a young woman who was very, very good at weaving. She was so good that she became known far and wide for her skill. People would visit just to watch her weave, and on one of those occasions, Arachne boasted that she was so good, it was as if she had been taught by Athena herself, though Athena would deny it. If we know anything about Greek mythology, it's that mortals should

never, ever compare themselves to the gods (the results were *always* disastrous). The goddess immediately heard of Arachne's claims and decided to visit her. Athena disguised herself as a fragile, elderly woman and visited Arachne to warn her against comparing herself to gods and goddesses, and suggested that she pray to the goddess to forgive her. In response, Arachne dug in to her earlier claims, saying she had no need for that kind of advice and the goddess herself should visit so they could have a contest! This was all it took for Athena to get angry and competitive: In an instant, she transformed herself back into her goddess form and agreed to the contest.

Athena and Arachne each wove incredible scenes, more impressive than anyone in attendance could imagine. Athena wove a scene of Athens with all the gods depicted in their glory. Arachne wove many smalls scenes, all showing instances when the gods had tricked, harmed, or punished humans for one thing or another. Most of the stories involved Athena's beloved father, Zeus, and the many times he had assaulted women, only to cause their ruin when he was finished. There was no question it was more impressive than what Athena had woven, but it also showed another level of pride. Arachne was calling out the gods for how they behaved, and Athena was not happy about it.

Athena was not only her father's favorite; she also had his temper. In response to Arachne's actions, Athena took the piece Arachne had woven and ripped it to shreds before taking Arachne's tools and destroying those as well. Arachne was so distraught by what Athena had done—in essence ruining all that Arachne was good at—she tried to kill herself. But Athena, finally feeling a little bit of sympathy for the woman, saved her at the last moment and instead transformed her into a spider.

Now You Know

The story of Athena and Arachne was said to explain the world's first spider, a creature that weaves intricate creations that can be so easily destroyed. *Arachne* means "spider" in ancient Greek and is where the word *arachnid* comes from.

APHRODITE

Goddess of Love, Beauty, and Sex

AKA: Venus (Roman/Latin); Cyprian Goddess

What's Her Deal?

Along with Athena, Aphrodite is one of the most famous of the Greek goddesses: Everyone knows the goddess of love! Aphrodite was renowned for her beauty (which she was very, very aware of) and her ability to elicit sexual desire. She was born off the island of Cyprus and was associated with it, often called the Cyprian Goddess. Some say she was born of the foam resulting from Ouranos's castration; others say she was actually the daughter of Zeus and the Titan Dione.

Aphrodite was *technically* married to the god Hephaestus, but it was not a happy marriage. She was married off to Hephaestus, very much against her wishes, when Zeus attempted to free Hera from Hephaestus's trap (see Hephaestus's entry). While married to Hephaestus, Aphrodite had affairs with, among others: Ares, Adonis, Hermes, Dionysus, and Poseidon. She and Ares were the parents of a number of children, including the goddess Harmonia (see Cadmus's entry) and, according to some traditions, Eros, the god of love and sexual desire. She and Ares were famously caught in a very sticky situation, an example of one of their many, many nights spent together (see Ares's entry for that entertaining and dramatic story).

While Aphrodite was the mother of a number of children, according to most mythological traditions, she and her husband, Hephaestus, didn't have *any* children together. She didn't really like her husband very much, but she was stuck with him.

The Story You Need to Know

The story of Aphrodite and Adonis is one of the most famous romances in mythology, though it's often more about Adonis as a concept than a character. The name *Adonis* has become synonymous with a beautiful, handsome man, an *Adonis*.

Adonis caught the eye of Aphrodite the moment he was born (we won't dig too deep into just how troubling that is). Aphrodite spotted the baby and knew that when he grew to be a man, she wanted him for herself. So she took him and brought him down to the Underworld, where she asked Persephone, goddess of spring and queen of the Underworld, to watch over him until he was grown. But Persephone also found herself falling for Adonis as he grew up, and she decided she wasn't about to give him over to Aphrodite.

Neither goddess would agree to give up her claim on Adonis, who, by this point, was, thankfully, a grown (if still young) man. The argument over him became so heated that Zeus was brought in to settle it. He determined that, much like Persephone, Adonis would spend a portion of his time with Aphrodite and a portion with Persephone, and, as a bonus, he would get a portion of time to spend by himself. Adonis, though, favored Aphrodite and chose to give up the time he had to spend by himself in order to spend more time with her.

When Adonis was with Aphrodite, she devoted herself to him. She brought him wherever he wanted to go and even agreed to do what he wanted. She went along with Adonis when he went hunting, something Aphrodite would never normally partake in. On one of those hunting trips, Adonis found himself face-to-face with a wild boar. He threw his spear, and though he hit the boar, it only served to make the animal angrier. Before Aphrodite could do anything to stop it, Adonis had been gored by the angry boar. Aphrodite reached him as he was dying and gave him one last kiss. Where Adonis's blood stained the forest floor grew deep-red flowers, anemones.

Another memorable lover of Aphrodite was the Trojan Anchises. She had bragged about not having children by a mortal, so Zeus caused her to lust after Anchises, a mortal. She became pregnant by him and gave birth to Aeneas, a prince of Troy who, according to Roman tradition, would go on to found Rome.

Now You Know

When Aphrodite and the god Hermes were together, they had a child named Hermaphroditus, whose name was a combination of both gods' names. When Hermaphroditus was grown, he had an encounter with a nymph, Salmacis, and the two were merged into one. According to Greek mythology, they became the first intersex person.

APOLLO

God of Music, Prophecy, Healing, and Plague

AKA: Apollon (alternate spelling); Phoebus Apollo (Greek and Roman/Latin)

What's His Deal?

Apollo was the god of music, prophecy, healing, and plague and was often called Phoebus Apollo (*phoebus* means "bright" and comes from his grandmother, the Titan Phoebe). He was also the twin brother to the goddess Artemis. Their mother was the Titan Leto, and the story of their birth is *dramatic* (more on that in Leto's entry). Though he was not one of the original Olympians who defeated the Titans, Apollo was one of the most important and famous of the Greek gods. Together, he and his sister were in charge of protecting children. He was in charge of protecting boys, while Artemis protected girls.

Apollo was one of the only Olympian gods who didn't get a new name when the Romans adapted the mythology of the Greeks. *Apollo* is *Apollo* in the Greek *and* the Latin.

Apollo's role in the world was wide ranging: As the god of music, he was associated with the nine Muses and was often shown carrying the lyre, an instrument of ancient Greece. Apollo was also the god of prophecy, so the famous Oracle of Delphi was dedicated to him. It was believed that the Pythia (the woman through which the Oracle acted) was speaking the word of Apollo himself. The ancient Greeks both in reality and mythology would travel miles and miles to visit the Oracle and ask her questions. In mythology, the running theme of the Oracle's prophecies was humans trying to avoid the fate foretold by the Oracle and, in doing so, inadvertently bringing about that exact fate. As the god of healing (and, similarly, of plague and illness), Apollo was in charge of medicine, which he bestowed upon the minor god Asclepius (the god of medicine) and his daughter Hygieia (the goddess of cleanliness and hygiene).

The Story You Need to Know

Hyacinthus was a young prince of Sparta, a grandson of the founder of Sparta himself. He was powerful and important, and he was *beautiful*. Hyacinthus was so beautiful that both the god Apollo and the god of the West Wind, Zephyr, fell completely in love with him. Hyacinthus, though, favored Apollo, and the two often spent time together. On one of these visits, the couple set out to play a game of discus (basically ancient Frisbee); although, according to the Roman poet Ovid, in order to play properly, they first had to strip naked and anoint themselves in oil. The game quickly became competitive, and they decided to see who could throw the discus farther.

Apollo threw the discus first. He was a god, so his throw was obviously impressive. The discus flew fast and far, and Hyacinthus ran to meet it, eager to catch it and show off his own skills by throwing it back to Apollo. But Zephyr, the West Wind, had been watching, and he was jealous of all the attention being paid to Apollo. Apollo was already a much more powerful god, so Zephyr couldn't bear to let him also have the man they both liked! While the discus was flying and Hyacinthus was running to catch it, Zephyr caused the wind to pick up. The wind threw the discus off course, and it hit Hyacinthus in the head. Poor Hyacinthus fell to the ground and was motionless.

Apollo rushed to his beloved Hyacinthus as he lay on the ground, but when he reached him, it was clearly too late. Blood gushed from the wound in Hyacinthus's head, and the life was already beginning to drain from him. So Apollo, in his grief, caused the blood on the grass to transform into deep purple flowers. Onto the petals of these new flowers Apollo inscribed the words *ai ai*, the sound of grief.

Now You Know

In later Greek mythology, Apollo became conflated with the Titan Helios, the god of the sun. This is why, even now, he is often shown driving the chariot that pulled the sun across the sky every day. Originally this was the job of Helios, but the characters of mythology dwindled over the generations, and Apollo eventually took on the role.

ARTEMIS

Goddess of the Hunt and Wilderness

AKA: Diana (Roman/Latin)

52525252

What's Her Deal?

Artemis was the twin sister of the god Apollo, and she was the goddess of the hunt and the wilderness. Artemis was born to Leto, once Leto had finally found a place where she could safely give birth (see Leto's entry for background). Once Leto had given birth to Artemis, the newly born goddess helped her mother through the labor of her own twin brother, Apollo, and therefore became associated with childbirth. The goddess also acted as the protectress of young girls, as her brother did for boys.

Artemis was famous for being a virgin goddess, shunning almost all contact with and attentions of men (see Actaeon's entry for the most famous instance of this!). Even the priestesses of Artemis's temples were bound to remain unmarried virgins, like the goddess. She was known to spend her time with a group of nymphs, and together they would hunt and wander the forests, bathe in the rivers and lakes, and generally revel in the outdoors. Artemis's weapon of choice was a bow and arrows, with which she was incredibly skilled. Artemis was typically shown dressed for hunting: She wore a short dress, carried her bow and arrow, and sometimes even had an animal pelt draped across her shoulder. She often rode in a chariot pulled by deer, galloping through the forest with her nymph entourage.

In an act quite out of character for Artemis, she required a human sacrifice by the Greeks before they could travel to the Trojan War. Agamemnon, the leader of the Greeks as they prepared to sail to war, had angered Artemis, and in order to please her he sacrificed his own daughter Iphigenia in one of the only instances of a human sacrifice to the gods.

The Story You Need to Know

Callisto was the daughter of a king named Lycaon and was one of the women who regularly accompanied the goddess Artemis on hunting trips. Because she was devoted to Artemis, Callisto had taken a vow of chastity and intended to remain an unmarried virgin. The two were very close friends and spent much of their time together among the wild beasts of the forests.

Tragically, on one of these trips into the forest, Callisto was noticed by Artemis's father, the king of the gods, Zeus. Zeus decided that he "loved" Callisto and that he must have her. Callisto, having vowed to remain a virgin, had no desire to ruin her friendship with Artemis, nor to be with Zeus in the first place. But Zeus wasn't concerned with things like that, and he assaulted Callisto. In order to do it, he transformed himself into Artemis so Callisto believed she was safe (Zeus could really be quite awful).

For some time, Callisto tried to hide Zeus's assault from her friend, pretending nothing had happened. She was hurt and ashamed at what Zeus had done to her. Eventually, though, it became clear that she was pregnant with Zeus's child. Zeus's wife, Hera, eventually found out the secret and transformed Callisto into a bear (sadly, there are a lot of stories in which women get punished by other women for what men did). In the form of a bear, Callisto gave birth to her son by Zeus (he was born a bear as well) and named him Arcas. But Hera wasn't finished with her horrific punishment. One day, when Artemis was out hunting, Hera pointed out the bear to suggest it as the next target for Artemis's arrows. Artemis hunted the bear and killed Callisto. When she realized what she'd done, she immortalized Callisto by placing her among the stars as the constellation Callisto the bear, or Ursa Major. At some point, Arcas, Callisto's son, was also placed in the stars as Ursa Minor (some versions suggest Arcas, as a human, was the one who hunted and killed Callisto).

Now You Know

Both of Artemis's sacred animals, the bear and the stag, are representative of mortals she harmed in one way or another. The bear, of course, comes from Callisto, whose fate Artemis felt guilty for, and the stag comes from the hunter Actaeon (whose story is told in his entry).

HEPHAESTUS

God of Fire, Craftsmanship, and Sculpture

AKA: Hephaistos (alternate spelling); Vulcan (Roman/Latin); Vulcanos

꧁꧂꧁꧂꧁꧂

What's His Deal?

Hephaestus was the god of fire and the forge, craftsmanship, and sculpture. He was an Olympian, born of the goddess Hera without the help of a man. Hera was furious with her husband, Zeus, for constantly cheating on her with other women, nymphs, and goddesses and, through those women, producing more and more children that weren't her own! Hera felt as if Zeus's escapades were being rubbed in her face all the time. Specifically, Hera felt that through the birth of Zeus's daughter Athena he had proven that he didn't need women at all! Truthfully, Metis was Athena's mother, but because Zeus "gave birth" to her himself (though, her bursting from his head isn't quite "giving birth"), he was really showing off. In order to get back at Zeus and prove she was just as capable as him, Hera gave birth to Hephaestus all by herself.

It's often tricky to make sense of the chronology in Greek mythology. Thousands of years and countless sources mean that not everything tracks in a linear fashion (like Hera giving birth to Hephaestus because she was mad about Zeus having Athena; meanwhile, Hephaestus also notoriously aided Zeus in the birth of Athena...).

Hephaestus was not considered one of the more attractive or appealing gods (a constant frustration for his wife, Aphrodite); in fact, he was the opposite. In Disney's *Hercules* (the 1998 TV series), however, Hephaestus is portrayed as a beefy, muscular god, whereas Ares (whom Aphrodite did find *very* attractive) is portrayed as quite the opposite.

The Story You Need to Know

When Hephaestus was born, Hera was less than thrilled by the outcome of her efforts to have a child without the help of a man. Hephaestus was born with a disability—one of his legs didn't work properly. Hera was so angry with Hephaestus's appearance that she threw him from Mount Olympus and out of her sight (yes, a cringeworthy reaction). He was found by the nymphs Thetis and Eurynome, who cared for Hephaestus and raised him far from Mount Olympus.

When Hephaestus was grown, he learned to become a skilled blacksmith and craftsman. In a show of affection to his distant mother, he built a golden throne for Hera and sent it up to Mount Olympus. But Hephaestus was still angry with Hera for what she'd done (how could he not be!), and the throne turned out to be a trap. The moment Hera sat down, the throne strapped her in, and not even Zeus could free her.

Zeus set out to have Hephaestus returned to Mount Olympus so that Hera could be freed from her throne. He decided this would be best done by bribing the god who brought him back. He proclaimed that whichever god returned Hephaestus to Mount Olympus would be given Aphrodite in marriage. At first, Aphrodite agreed to this, but only because she assumed that Ares, the god she loved, would be the one able to bring Hephaestus back. But Ares failed—Hephaestus easily beat back his attempts at restraint.

Hephaestus now knew what was going on. He was next approached by Dionysus, who was never one to follow the rules. Dionysus suggested that Hephaestus simply return himself to Olympus. He would be able to gain his seat with the gods, *and* he would get to marry the most beautiful goddess, the goddess of love, beauty, and sex herself, Aphrodite. Hephaestus did exactly that: He surrendered himself to Zeus and Hera on Mount Olympus, he freed Hera, and he married Aphrodite.

Even though Hephaestus and Aphrodite were married, they never had any children together, and Aphrodite frequently cheated on Hephaestus with Ares and other gods. With Ares, she had many children. Aphrodite had been forced to marry Hephaestus, and she never let him forget it.

Now You Know

The stories surrounding Hephaestus usually involve him crafting various means of tricking and trapping gods and goddesses who have wronged him in some way. Another impressive (and entertaining!) example of this is found in the entry on Ares.

ARES

God of War, Courage, and Civil Order
AKA: Mars (Roman/Latin)

ᓫᓫᓫᓫᓫᓫᓫ

What's His Deal?

Ares was the god of war, known for his role in riling up men on
both sides of battles. While he was an important god, Ares doesn't
appear in many stories. Primarily, he's involved with Aphrodite,
the goddess he loved but lost in marriage to Hephaestus. Together they had a number of children: Harmonia, the goddess of harmony; Phobos and Deimos, the personifications of terror and fear;
and (according to some sources) Eros, the god of love and sexual
desire.

A lost satirical play by Aeschylus features Sisyphus escaping his eternal punishment in the Underworld only to kidnap the god of death, Thanatos, before being caught by Ares, who returned both to their rightful places.

Ares was always depicted with his warrior's helmet, either wearing it or holding it, and often appears in pop culture representations of Greek mythology: He's the main villain in the 2017 DC movie *Wonder Woman* and features in the films *Wrath of the Titans* (2012) and *Immortals* (2011). He's also an important character in the first Percy Jackson novel. Like Hades, Ares is often portrayed as a villain in pop culture but was rarely, if ever, the villain in mythology. The portrayal of Ares in *Lore Olympus* is one of the most accurate in pop culture; he's a god of war, but he isn't necessarily a bad guy.

The Story You Need to Know

Ares and Aphrodite often found ways to spend time together, despite Aphrodite being married to Hephaestus. They loved each other, and the fact that she had been forced to marry a man she didn't love seemed to give them both the confidence to do what they wanted, no matter how risky. On one of these occasions, Ares and Aphrodite slept together in her and Hephaestus's home in their shared bed. They may have done this before, but this time Ares stayed too long. He stayed long enough that Helios had begun to bring the chariot of the sun across the sky. From above,

Helios saw the couple together and went immediately to tell Hephaestus what he'd seen.

Hephaestus, whether or not he knew about their relationship before this, was furious that they'd been seen together, and in his own bed! He went straight to his forge and began to devise a way of punishing Ares and Aphrodite. Hephaestus created a set of magical chains: They were lightweight and completely invisible, and would do exactly what he wanted them to. He draped them around his bed and hung them from the ceiling. With his trap set, Hephaestus pretended to head off to the island of Lemnos, saying he wouldn't be back for a couple of days, and with that he left Aphrodite alone in their home.

The moment Hephaestus left, Ares was in the door and with Aphrodite. He was always aware of when he might have the chance to be with her without Hephaestus nearby. The couple went immediately to the bed and lay down. In an instant, the chains sprang into action, winding their way around the couple, securing them to the bed in exactly the position they'd lain down in.

Once Ares and Aphrodite were chained to the bed, unable to move, Hephaestus returned (once again, Helios had seen them and told the god). Before he entered the home, though, he called to the other gods to come and witness what he was about to reveal. Zeus and all the other Olympians arrived at the scene. Hephaestus was distraught, angry, and yelling about the adulterous pair and how they'd shamed him. The other gods, though, couldn't contain their laughter when they saw Ares and Aphrodite there, chained to the bed, annoyed and very guilty.

Hephaestus went on about how he didn't intend to release the couple from the chains, but Poseidon attempted to convince him to let them go. Poseidon insisted that he himself would make sure that Ares paid for his crimes. Finally, Hephaestus relented, not able to say no to Poseidon, and he let the couple go. Embarrassed and frustrated, Ares immediately went off to Thrace while Aphrodite hid away on Cyprus.

Now You Know

Ares was close with the goddess Eris, the goddess of strife and discord (her Roman/Latin name is Discordia). Eris was famous for her role in starting the Trojan War (see Paris's entry) and for her love of rampaging through battlefields, crying out for bloodshed. They often rode through the Trojan War together, though Eris's love of violence overshadowed even that of Ares.

HERMES

God of Herds and Flocks, Travelers, Trade, Writing, Athleticism, and Astronomy;
the Messenger God

AKA: Mercury; Mercurius (both Roman/Latin)

꙰꙰꙰꙰꙰

What's His Deal?

Hermes was a god of many things in addition to serving as the Olympians' second messenger (the other was a goddess named Iris). For example, he inhabited the role of "trickster god," a common trope among ancient mythologies. Hermes was the child of Zeus and the nymph Maia, one of the Pleiades (sisters who were eventually placed in the sky as the constellation with the same name). You probably remember him from Disney's *Hercules*, in which he's the cool, fast-talking, sunglasses-wearing companion and messenger of Zeus.

The Story You Need to Know

The god Hermes was born to Maia in a cave on Mount Kyllene. She was a private woman who didn't want to associate with many of the gods. She did like Zeus, though (at least, it seems like it; it's one of the rare instances when a woman returned his interest). She and Zeus used to spend time together in the dead of night, when Hera was soundly sleeping on Mount Olympus.

Hermes was born in the morning, and it's said that by lunchtime he had invented the lyre and by the afternoon he had escaped his cradle and planned to steal Apollo's cattle. Keep in mind he was a literal *baby*; this was the *same day* he was born. The invention of the lyre happened because the baby Hermes was distracted by a tortoise the moment he left his mother's cave. Hermes found this tortoise simply hilarious (again, he was a baby). He told the tortoise all about his plans for the animal, what it would represent, that he would make it *sing*! Then he killed it, cut off its limbs, and hollowed out its shell, to which he attached various strings and reeds, thus inventing the lyre. And it was only midday! He had so much of the day left, so he decided to steal Apollo's cattle.

The baby Hermes crossed a swath of Greece to reach Pieria, where Apollo kept his cattle. Hermes found them grazing happily, sneaked in, and removed them all and began to walk them to another region entirely. He disguised their tracks by walking backward so that it would look as though he were walking with the animals in the opposite direction. Apollo had no idea! Hermes walked the cattle all over Greece, encountering only one man, who was tending to his vineyard. Hermes asked the man to keep his secret, before finally sacrificing two of the cattle and eating his fill. Hermes was all about the thrill! Once this was done, he hid the rest of the cows and returned to his mother's cave as though nothing at all had happened.

Meanwhile, Apollo was looking high and low for his cattle. He came upon the man in his vineyard and asked if he'd seen anyone suspicious with cattle recently. The man, not as surprised as he should have been, told Apollo plainly that he'd seen an infant with cattle only just the other day. As soon as Apollo heard this story, he saw an omen that told him it was most definitely a child of Zeus who had done this, but still he didn't know who! Hermes was so young that the other Olympians didn't know he even existed. Apollo followed the tracks and whatever other clues he could find along the way, and finally, after so much searching and many dead ends, he ended up at the cave on Mount Kyllene.

When Hermes saw Apollo at the mouth of the cave, he curled himself up as small as he could, hiding in his swaddling clothes. Apollo searched the whole of the cave before finally finding the baby and calling him out, asking where his cattle were. Apollo threatened to send Hermes to the Underworld itself if he didn't reveal the location of the cattle! First Hermes feigned ignorance, saying he didn't know anything about Apollo's cows, but eventually Zeus was brought in to settle the matter between his two sons. He brought the two to Olympus, where they made their cases, Hermes still denying all (and still *a baby*!). In time he cracked, and Hermes brought Zeus and Apollo to the spot where he had hidden the rest of the cattle. Apollo was happy to have them returned, though he was furious (and baffled) that Hermes had killed two of them, all *as a baby*.

Now You Know

After Hermes killed the giant beloved by Hera, Argus Panoptes, in an effort to free the Naiad Io, he gained the epithet Argeiphontes ("Slayer of Argus").

DIONYSUS

God of Theater, Wine, Vegetation, Pleasure, and Madness

AKA: Bacchus (Greek and Roman/Latin); Liber (Roman/Latin)

ᔕᔑᔕᔑᔕᔑᔕᔑ

What's His Deal?

Dionysus was the fun god, the party god. He was the god of many things, but most importantly of wine, pleasure, and theater. Dionysus was the only Olympian born to a mortal woman, Semele. This makes him one of the descendants of Cadmus, the founder of Thebes, and so he was associated with that city's history as well as the family curse, though he was unaffected by it. Simultaneously, Dionysus was often described as a god who returned to the Greek world from the east. Even still, there is evidence that Dionysus was actually one of the first gods worshipped in the Greek world, appearing in writings from the earliest languages of the Greeks. He was also worshipped the longest; as the Roman god Liber, worship of Dionysus extended beyond the reach of most of the other Olympian gods. Dionysus was often depicted as a young gender-fluid individual, carrying a glass for drinking wine and his thyrsus, a reed staff.

There's enough to say about Dionysus to fill multiple books, though his worship varied greatly in its presentation. Put simply, though, he was a god of the people, one regular humans could relate to more than the other Olympians. This manifested in his symbols of wine and theatrical performance.

The Story You Need to Know

The story of Dionysus's return to Greece is most famously told in the Greek tragedy *The Bacchae* by Euripides. The god Dionysus arrived in Thebes, the city of his birth, disguised as one of his own priests. With him were the Maenads (also called Bacchae), a group of women devoted to worshipping Dionysus. In Thebes he found Pentheus, his cousin and the current king, who was actively denouncing the god, telling the people of Thebes not to worship this new god and threatening punishment if they did. He and others refused to acknowledge that Dionysus was a god, one born of their own family member Semele (and Zeus).

Dionysus also features as a character in Aristophanes's comedic play *The Frogs*, in which Dionysus travels into the Underworld and holds a competition between two deceased tragedians, Aeschylus and Euripides. The two dead playwrights fight over who was the best at writing tragedy, quoting themselves and their characters and debating what makes a good play. Plus, there is a chorus of singing frogs!

Pentheus's mother and Dionysus's aunt, Agave, among other women of Thebes, became involved with the group worshipping Dionysus. She and many other Theban women retreated into the nearby forests, where they partied *hard*. They drank wine and danced and sang and ripped animals to shreds (it's a Maenad thing). Pentheus found out about these acts and was horrified, so he planned to send soldiers in to kill all the women worshipping Dionysus—even Pentheus's own mother. Their actions were so against the norm that Pentheus believed they should adhere to that, in his mind, they deserved death. Dionysus, though, still in disguise, persuaded Pentheus that this wasn't yet necessary. He instead suggested that he should spy on the women while disguised as one of them. Pentheus, at this point himself descending into Dionysian madness, agreed to this plan and dressed himself like one of the women, a Maenad, following Dionysus into the forests to spy on the Theban women in their wine-filled frenzy.

When Pentheus arrived at the spot in the forest where the women were gathered, he was still in his crazed state and decided it would be best if he climbed to the top of one of the trees so he could look down on the women from above. Once he did this, Dionysus revealed himself and pointed out Pentheus to the Maenads. This action by Dionysus drove the Maenads completely mad, and they pulled Pentheus down from the tree and proceeded to rip him limb from limb.

When it was all over, Agave returned to the city of Thebes, holding her son's head in her hands. She believed it was the head of a lion and said that she was able to defeat the lion herself. She was proud, showing off. Agave's madness eventually began to wear off, and her father, Cadmus, revealed to her what she'd actually done.

Now You Know

Dionysus was the god of theater, so Greek drama was dedicated to him. The main event where ancient Greek plays were performed was the Dionysia, an annual festival held in Athens where three playwrights would compete for the top prize. It always began with a sacrifice to Dionysus and included a procession of *phalloi* (yes, phallic statues) that traveled all through the city.

HESTIA

Goddess of the Hearth and Home
AKA: Vesta (Roman/Latin)

᠎᠎᠎᠎᠎᠎᠎

What's Her Deal?

Hestia was a virgin goddess and one of the most important gods of daily life in ancient Greece. As the goddess of the hearth and home, she was worshipped daily and was responsible for domestic life and, as such, domestic happiness. In this role, she received a portion of all sacrifices made to the gods. When the ancient Greeks sacrificed an animal to the gods, they would prepare a feast with the remaining portion, which was presided over by Hestia. All ancient cities and towns would also have a public hearth sacred to Hestia, the fire at which was never permitted to go out.

Hestia was both the oldest and youngest of the Olympians: She was the firstborn of Kronos and Rhea and therefore the first eaten by Kronos. Because of this she was the last to be vomited up by him upon his defeat by Zeus. This made Hestia and Zeus both the youngest and oldest children.

Hestia kept herself free of the drama that the other gods fed off of daily. She didn't involve herself with humans or even the other gods. There was a brief time when both Apollo and Poseidon sought to marry Hestia, but she made it very clear to them, and to Zeus, that she wouldn't be marrying anyone and that she would remain a virgin. For likely the same reason—a complete disinterest in the other Olympian gods—Hestia was only sometimes considered one of the Olympians, though she retained her importance in the lives of the Greeks.

The Story You Need to Know

Hestia remained so far removed from the other gods that there are no stories associated with her (at least, none that have survived the millennia). She was more important historically than she was mythologically; as the goddess of the home, the ancient Greeks relied on her for everything to do with their homes and the safety and comfort that came with them.

Ovid, the Roman poet, relates the only incident involving Hestia and the gods. She attended a feast where the gods mingled with nymphs and satyrs. Hestia took a short nap, and while she was asleep, the god Priapus got it into his head that he was going to assault her. A nearby donkey brayed loudly, causing Hestia to wake up before he was able to do anything, and he found himself very embarrassed for the whole event.

Now You Know

The Romans eventually adapted the cult of worship of Hestia. Her Roman/Latin name was Vesta, and the Romans had a group of specially selected girls called the Vestal Virgins, who were devoted to Vesta and maintained the sacred fire burning in her sanctuaries. These girls were some of the most important priestesses in the Roman world.

PART 3

DEITIES, ETC.

The pantheon of Greek mythology contains countless types of humanlike beings. This section includes the characters of varying levels of divinity: the beings who are not simply mortals, or even heroes, but are also not among the main gods ruling from Mount Olympus. These are the stories of Titans, nymphs, lesser gods, and even monsters.

The Olympian gods discussed in Part 2 also feature in most of the stories in this section, but it's the non-Olympian deities who are the most important characters here: the good, the bad, and the monstrous. These characters have important and iconic stories that revolve less around the Olympians and more around the dramatic and tragic lives of other divine beings. There is the Titan who gave humanity fire and was punished for it; there is the Titan-mother of the Olympian twins, pursued by a vengeful goddess; there is a nymph ruined by a god but able to make a beautiful thing as a result; there is the god of love who fell in love; there is the origin of echoes and narcissists; and there are the monstrous parents of all the most exciting Greek mythological creatures. The stories of these non-Olympian deities (a term used broadly here to mean those who are divine in some way and who are not human) are some of the most iconic, important, and well known of Greek mythology. As a bonus, the monsters (and their equally monstrous children) are freaky and fascinating.

PROMETHEUS

A Titan; God of Forethought

What's His Deal?

Prometheus and his brother Epimetheus (the god of afterthought) were two of the Titans who sided with the Olympian gods in their war against many of the other Titans, the Titanomachy. Prometheus is famous not only for gifting humans with fire but also for tricking Zeus into allowing them to retain the best cuts of sacrificial meat for themselves. He was the god of forethought. Prometheus was the forward thinker in the family, the one who really thought out his actions before doing anything. (His brother was quite the opposite.)

According to some versions of the origin of humanity, men were created by Prometheus and Epimetheus, a task assigned to them by the gods. But Epimetheus was not very good at such things, and so he gave away all the meaningful traits to the animals, leaving none left for humans (fur, scales, and camouflage were all taken!). Prometheus, feeling bad for the new humans, who had no protection, chose to bestow upon humanity the ability to walk upright, one of the only things he could think of to give people the upper hand over the animals, and the means to create fire.

Prometheus features in Madeline Miller's novel *Circe*, in which the titular witch encounters him in his punishment, chained to a rock. Her experience with him induces an appreciation of humans that only Prometheus could convey.

The Story You Need to Know

While the story of who created *man*kind varies in Greek mythology, it's agreed that in the beginning there were only men. These men did not inherently have the ability to create fire. The bestowing of the gift of fire to the first men was done by the Titan Prometheus. Prometheus stole the fire from Mount Olympus itself, hiding it in a fennel stalk and bringing it in secret to the humans, very much against the will of Zeus, who would have preferred the humans to be much more helpless.

Prometheus had a special affection for people, perhaps because he created them. He appreciated them in a way that the other gods did not—for example, Zeus thought them a nuisance. Not only did Prometheus gift the new humans with fire; he also tricked Zeus into allowing them to sacrifice the worst meat to the gods while keeping the best for themselves. Prometheus cut up an ox into pieces, taking all the most disgusting, least edible parts and wrapping them in fat. He then took the most edible, most appealing parts and wrapped them up in the leftover skin of the animals. Prometheus then presented the two options to Zeus, asking which he would prefer the humans sacrifice to the gods and which they should keep for themselves. Of course, Zeus selected the most appealing-looking package: the nasty parts wrapped up in nice-looking fat.

The ancient Greeks took sacrifices *very* seriously. Animals (usually cattle or oxen) were sacrificed before festivals and any other time the Greeks felt the gods needed to be appeased. Because of Prometheus, the resulting feasts included much better meat, and the humans were able to enjoy it equally themselves!

Zeus was furious with Prometheus for this trick, so he promised vengeance on both Prometheus and the humans Prometheus had insisted on helping at the expense of the gods. First, he punished the humans (that story is told in Pandora's entry). Once the humans were sufficiently punished, according to Zeus, he set his eyes upon Prometheus. Because Prometheus had helped Zeus in his war against the other Titans, Zeus probably should have owed him…but Zeus wasn't concerned with that. He was far too frustrated with Prometheus's love for the humans and his incessant need to help them.

In retribution for Prometheus's acts of charity toward the humans, Zeus had him seized and brought to the Caucasus Mountains. There, Prometheus was chained to a rock, and once he was securely fastened, Zeus sent an eagle (his own symbolic animal) to peck at Prometheus's stomach, eventually pecking out the Titan's liver in the most excruciating way imaginable. Overnight, Prometheus healed (a trait of his Titan status), just in time for the eagle to arrive the next morning and repeat the actions. This happened, day after day, for generations, until finally Heracles arrived and freed Prometheus from this perpetual punishment.

Now You Know

The subtitle to Mary Shelley's novel *Frankenstein* is *The Modern Prometheus*, a reference to how her character Dr. Frankenstein is a creator of humanity who was subsequently harmed by his own creation, similar to the Titan Prometheus's punishment for bestowing fire upon the humans. It's theorized that her subtitle could also have been referencing the morality of meat-eating, since Prometheus introduced the concept to humans and Shelley was an avowed vegetarian!

Pandora

The First Woman

———◆——

Pandora was the world's first woman, according to Greek mythology. She was bestowed upon the existing men as both a gift and a curse. There are two versions of the story of Pandora that are equally worth telling. The first continues on from the story of Prometheus: Zeus was angry with the Titan for gifting the humans (which at that time consisted of only men) with fire stolen from Olympus and the choice cuts of meat during a sacrifice. He

sought to punish both the humans and Prometheus. His punishment directed at the humans was, simply, the creation of women (an old and very hurtful trope!). Zeus directed the god Hephaestus to create the first woman out of clay. Pandora, this first woman, was beautiful, shining, and glorious. Zeus had the other gods grant her both gifts and faults: Athena taught her to weave, Aphrodite made her graceful, and Hermes made her deceitful. In this version of the story, however, she was also simply evil and thus so were all the women who descended from her. This is not the most sympathetic story, nor is it one that explains all the magnificent women of Greek mythology (not to mention it's sexist).

The second story of Pandora is *slightly* less hateful toward all women. It begins as the other does, with Zeus seeking to punish Prometheus for the theft of fire from the Olympians, and with Hephaestus being directed to create Pandora. Pandora (who in this telling is not the embodiment of all evil and therefore neither are all women) was given a jar (more commonly known as a box) and expressly instructed not to open it. She was then brought to the Titan Epimetheus and given to him as a new wife. Epimetheus had been instructed by his brother Prometheus not to accept any gifts of the gods, but since Epimetheus was the god of afterthought, he'd promptly forgotten this advice. Epimetheus and Pandora were married, and before long, Pandora became curious about the contents of the jar she'd been given by the gods. She was curious, as many intelligent people are, and sought to learn what was inside. She opened the jar, and it released all the horrors, plagues, and evils into the world. Realizing what she'd done, she closed the jar as quickly as she could. What was left inside was only hope, leaving it as humankind's one defense and comfort against the problems of the world.

According to this version of the story, women aren't inherently evil; they are just so naturally curious as to accidentally inflict the world's evils upon humankind. Neither story is particularly sympathetic toward women, but both are indicative of the way the ancient Greeks felt about women in general. Fortunately, Pandora is also associated with hope, and its importance in the lives of humans was emphasized strongly.

LETO

A Titan; Goddess of Motherhood; Protector of the Young

AKA: Latona (Roman/Latin)

〰️〰️〰️〰️

What's Her Deal?

Leto was a Titan and the goddess of motherhood. Alongside her children, Artemis and Apollo, Leto was a protector of the young. She was the daughter of the Titans Coeus (the god of *rational* intellect) and Phoebe (the goddess of *bright, shining* intellect) and the mother of two of the most important gods of Greece (though Apollo far outweighed his sister in that respect). What made Phoebe's intellect bright and shining isn't entirely clear, but she was associated with oracular, prophetic intellect, whereas Coeus's intellect was more down to earth.

Early on in the story of the Titans, gods, and Olympians, Zeus and Leto were together. Whether this was a relationship of love and affection or one of Zeus's many assaults is unclear—but, in any case, Leto became pregnant with twins. Before long, Hera found out about Zeus and Leto, and Leto's pregnancy, and she was furious. Hera swore she'd prevent Leto from giving birth in whatever way she could. Hera could be absolutely terrifying when she wanted to be (and she often wanted to be, while punishing women Zeus involved himself with), and because of this no one wanted to anger her.

Leto wandered aimlessly in search of somewhere she could give birth. She traveled through Greece and much of Asia Minor, but no one would welcome her. This may have been because people worried that it would anger Hera to allow Leto to give birth in their area, or it could have been a more finite, magical means of physically preventing Leto from giving birth. Finally, in all her searching, Leto came upon a floating island (it was believed that this island was not attached to the earth; instead it floated through the sea, unmoored). Leto was able to give birth on the island purely because it was not attached to the earth like the rest of the world she'd traveled. It was free of Hera's curse.

Leto gave birth first to the goddess Artemis, who then helped her mother give birth to her own twin brother, Apollo. Because of this, Artemis became a goddess of childbirth. Once Apollo was born, the island became sacred to him. It was renamed Delos (this island is incredibly important in the history of ancient Greece, and it was sacred long before it was attributed as the twins' birthplace). Together, the family of three gods were the protectors of the young.

The Story You Need to Know

Niobe was a mortal woman famous for having fourteen children. Her brother was a man named Pelops (see the entry on Tantalus and His Family for more). She lived in Thebes, where she married the king Amphion. With Amphion, Niobe had seven daughters and seven sons. Niobe was very proud of her children, both as people and the sheer volume of them! Once, while discussing her children and her own achievement in giving birth to *fourteen* of them, Niobe compared herself to Leto. She noted that she had fourteen children, while the goddess of motherhood only had two. Niobe felt herself far superior to Leto in this respect. Making this statement out loud was a *big mistake*.

The comparison (placing herself favorably above a goddess, and not just *any* goddess, but Leto) was overheard by the gods. Leto, Artemis, and Apollo were absolutely furious that Niobe would compare herself to Leto, as though she was better because she had more children! (Mortals should *never* compare themselves to gods...it results in so many tragedies.) The gods didn't wait for apologies. In their anger, Artemis and Apollo took aim at Niobe's children (both the twins were known for their archery skills). Artemis killed all seven of Niobe's daughters, and Apollo killed all seven of her sons (though some versions of the story leave one daughter and one son living). Niobe's children were left unburied for many days, as Zeus, adding to the woman's punishment, had turned the other Thebans to stone.

Niobe was so heartbroken by the death of all her children that eventually she, too, was transformed into a rock, though hers was a "weeping" rock, one from which water seeped.

Now You Know

Leto's sister was a Titan named Asteria, who was the mother of the witch goddess Hecate with the Titan Perses. Asteria was also pursued by Zeus (the list is endless!), but she managed to escape his grasp by transforming herself into a quail. Another telling of Leto arriving on the island of Delos says that Asteria, after becoming a quail, then jumped into the sea to escape Zeus further. While in the water, she was transformed into the island, which was then renamed Delos when Apollo was born on it.

DAPHNE

A Nymph

What's Her Deal?

Daphne was a Naiad, a nymph of freshwater fountains, who caught the attention of the god Apollo. She was a huntress, similar to Artemis. She loved to adventure in the woods and didn't care what men thought of her. She is often depicted in art—the most famous (and beautiful!) of which is Bernini's sculpture *Apollo and Daphne*. In Disney's *Hercules*, an unnamed nymph transforms herself into a tree in order to get away from Hercules's friend and trainer, Phil. Although the character is not named Daphne in the movie, this scene is certainly inspired by her story.

The Story You Need to Know

As a nymph, Daphne spent most of her time in the forest. She was there one day, minding her business and enjoying the outdoors, when she was spotted by Apollo. According to the Roman poet Ovid's version of the story, which is more detailed than the original Greek, Apollo had just had an argument with Eros, the god of love. Apollo had bragged to Eros about his skills with a bow and arrow, weapons that were symbolic to Apollo. But Eros was also skilled with a bow and arrow, though his arrows were tipped with either a love potion or what we'll call a "loathe potion." So when Apollo went on and on that day about how much better he was with a bow and arrow, Eros proved his own skills by shooting an arrow tipped with love potion at Apollo and one tipped with the loathe potion at Daphne.

The moment Apollo was hit with the arrow, he fell deeply, violently in love with Daphne, who just happened to be nearby when all of this was happening. When she was hit, she felt an immediate hatred of Apollo and wanted to be rid of him as quickly and completely as possible. She ran and he followed. Daphne ran through the forest as fast as she could, jumping over rocks and dodging tree branches, and all the while Apollo followed, keeping pace.

As they ran, Apollo yelled ahead to Daphne, trying to convince her to slow down and give him a chance. He told her how much he loved her and why (though he didn't mention Eros's arrow). He told her that while he wasn't as connected with the forest as she was, he was a god, the son of Zeus, and the god of the Oracle! He kept trying to convince her, naming every impressive thing he could think of. There was a lot too; Apollo was an impressive god. But not only had Daphne been hit with Eros's loathe arrow; she also had no desire for marriage even before being hit with it.

She enjoyed her freedom, being able to wander the forests and hunting for as long as she wanted.

Finally, Daphne became sick of running. She called to her father, a river god, asking him to help her escape this god's grasp (or, in some versions, she calls out to Gaia, Mother Earth herself). Her wish was granted: As soon as she wished it, she stopped in her tracks and began to transform. Bark started to grow on her skin, spreading quickly. Next, her feet sprouted roots, and her arms extended into branches. Just as Apollo reached Daphne, she completed her transformation, becoming the laurel tree. Apollo hugged and kissed the laurel tree, telling Daphne that he would love her always and that now she would be *his* tree. He just could not take the hint.

Once Daphne was transformed into a laurel tree, Apollo took it as his sacred plant. This is where the practice of wearing a crown of laurel comes from. It began with Apollo as a symbol of victory and spread into later Roman times.

Now You Know

In Greek mythology, Daphne was often seen as Apollo's bride. Their story wasn't viewed as particularly problematic because he loved her. Because of the status of women as the property of men, it was seen as a beautiful story in which Apollo got his sacred tree, rather than a story where a woman was forced to transform herself into an object in order to escape a man's clutches.

EROS

God of Erotic Love and Sex

AKA: Cupid (Roman/Latin)

What's His Deal?

Eros was the son of Aphrodite and Ares (alternately, he's sometimes described as a child of only Chaos itself!), a couple who were never officially together but who created some of the most memorable children of Greek mythology. Eros was the god of *erotic* love, whereas his mother, Aphrodite, was the goddess of love in general. Eros was perhaps better known by his Roman name, Cupid, although this character became associated more with childlike cherubs than the grown man of Greek mythology.

Representations of Eros in art are somewhat unique: The god is regularly depicted both as an adult (usually in a romantic embrace with his beloved Psyche) and as a child in the form of the typical cherubic Cupid figure.

Eros was famous for his bow and arrows, arrows that were tipped either with an incredibly potent love potion or an equally potent potion that convinced its victims that they absolutely *hated* the first person they saw. With these tools, Eros had great power, though it was most often used for comedic effect.

Now You Know

Eros is best known for his love of a woman named Psyche, though this story appears only in a Roman work of literature: Apuleius's *The Golden Ass* (also known as *Metamorphoses*). Theirs is a unique story; it's rare that a myth appears only in one source and gains the fame that this one did. Because their story was told by a Roman, the Roman names for the gods are used in the following entry.

Psyche

A Princess; Later, the Goddess of the Soul

———◆———

Psyche was a princess of an unnamed kingdom—Apuleius, her storyteller, didn't bother himself with those details. In the story, Psyche's most important attribute was her beauty, which brought suitors from all the ancient world. Once she married Cupid, she became a goddess herself and took the role of goddess of the soul (the *psyche*).

She is often depicted in art as having butterfly wings, while Cupid has angel wings. The most famous artistic rendering of Cupid and Psyche is the sculpture *Psyche Revived by Cupid's Kiss* by Antonio Canova, of which there are two versions. The original is in the Louvre in Paris, and Psyche doesn't have any wings; however, a second version resides in the Metropolitan Museum of Art in New York City, and in that version, Psyche has butterfly wings. The story of Cupid and Psyche features in an ongoing storyline in the Webtoon *Lore Olympus*. It's also retold in a novel by C.S. Lewis called *Till We Have Faces*.

The Story You Need to Know

Psyche was a princess so beautiful that she gained attention far beyond her own kingdom. People traveled from all over to see this woman, who was described as more beautiful than Venus (Aphrodite), the *goddess of beauty*. Psyche, to her credit, wasn't particularly interested in any of this comparing. But Venus saw what was happening and was absolutely infuriated. Nobody could be more beautiful than Venus; it was simply not possible. In her anger, she sent her son Cupid down to earth to punish Psyche for what was being said about her. He was to shoot Psyche with one of his arrows when she was near the most horrible creature imaginable—that way, she would fall in love with a monster (human or otherwise), not with one of her many attractive suitors.

Cupid traveled to earth intending to do exactly as his mother asked of him, but instead, when he saw Psyche, he found himself more attracted to her than anyone he'd ever seen before. He was completely in love and couldn't bring himself to ruin her as his mother wanted. Instead, Cupid brought Psyche away to a palace in the forest where they could live together in secret. But there was a hitch: She couldn't set eyes on him (while not always the case, it's generally understood that humans can't look upon gods in their natural form). When this was being planned, Psyche believed she was to be sacrificed, given in "marriage" to a monster in order to appease the goddess Venus. She was brought to a cliffside by her parents and two sisters in a procession and left there. Cupid, though, arranged for the West Wind, Zephyr, to whisk Psyche off the cliffside and down to the palace. When Psyche arrived, she was very confused, as this wasn't exactly what she'd expected....Where was the monster? The palace was beautiful and luxurious, but there didn't seem to be anyone there.

That night, Psyche was finally visited by the individual who told her he was to be her husband. She couldn't see his face; she could only hear his voice in the dark. This happened every night, and Psyche grew to love her new husband, even if she hadn't seen his face. Eventually, though, she started getting lonely. She convinced her husband to allow her to invite her sisters to the palace (she had no idea where she was, so she really needed his

help). When her sisters visited, they convinced Psyche that she must be married to a monster, and that's why she wasn't allowed to see his face. They convinced her he must be a monster if he was hiding from her and that she must bring a knife and a lamp in the night and shine a light to see what he really looked like, before killing him and escaping his palace.

That night, Psyche did as her sisters had suggested. Armed with a knife, she shone the lamp in front of her sleeping husband and was absolutely shocked to see that he wasn't a monster at all; instead he was the most beautiful man she'd ever seen: He was the god of *love* and *sex*! Before Psyche could fully appreciate how great this was, the oil from the lamp dripped onto her husband and burned him. He woke up, shocked; afraid of the knife in her hand; and very, very angry. He immediately fled, leaving Psyche alone in the palace.

Psyche was, of course, incredibly ashamed of what she'd done (not to mention upset that she'd ruined an awesome situation: a palace *and* the god of love!). She wandered in search of Cupid and tried to think of some way to reach him. She went from temple to temple before finally reaching the temple of Venus. This was a mistake. Venus knew immediately who she was and blamed her for what she described as the maiming of her son (in truth, it was a pretty minor burn). Venus trapped Psyche there, torturing her horribly before forcing her to begin a set of increasingly difficult and frustrating labors in retribution for her actions. Meanwhile, Psyche was still unable to contact Cupid. She knew that if she could just talk to him, she might be able to convince him that she really did love him and hadn't meant to distrust or hurt him. As she got further into the labors, though, Psyche was secretly helped by Cupid, who came to her invisibly, pushing her through the tasks assigned by Venus (which included sorting through millions of seeds and grains, gathering golden wool from angry and violent sheep, and collecting water from the rivers of the Underworld).

Psyche powered through, proving to Venus that she did truly love Cupid and wanted to make up for what she'd done. Once she'd completed the last of Venus's trials, Venus had to admit defeat. Psyche was reunited with Cupid and was brought to Mount Olympus, where she was made immortal (one of the rare instances of this happening to a human), becoming the goddess of the soul, the psyche.

The story of Psyche overcoming Venus's trials is a story of human perseverance and humanity's ability to overcome and make amends for mistakes made. It's also a rare instance of a real love story with a happy ending.

ECHO and NARCISSUS

A Nymph and a Young Mortal Man (the Son of a River God and a Nymph)

᠎᠎᠎᠎᠎

What's Their Deal?

Echo was a mountain nymph (an Oread) who spent her time in the company of other nymphs on Mount Cithaeron in Boeotia. These nymphs, however, were more concerned with Zeus than they were with Artemis. Narcissus was a beautiful young man, the son of a river god and a nymph, though he didn't seem to have inherited any of his parents' divinity. Though their story is more tragic than romantic, the pair are regularly depicted in art.

The Story You Need to Know

Echo was a nymph who spent a good deal of her time talking. She would visit with the other nymphs, and she also played a role in their (and Zeus's) private lives. Zeus enjoyed spending time with the nymphs of Mount Cithaeron, and those nymphs equally enjoyed Zeus's presence with them. But they were all aware of Hera's tendency toward checking in on her husband and punishing those he associated with. This was where Echo came in: When Zeus was off with her friends, the other nymphs, Echo would take it upon herself to distract Hera. Echo would chat and chat, keeping Hera busy and giving Zeus and the nymphs the opportunity to extricate themselves from whatever situation they may have been in before Hera could find them. Eventually, Hera found out what Echo was up to and punished her by making it so that Echo could only ever repeat what had just been said to her. She couldn't speak without someone else having spoken first, and she couldn't keep silent if someone said something around her. It was *frustrating*.

While cursed this way, Echo came upon the young man Narcissus. Narcissus was beautiful and handsome...and he knew it. Narcissus was notorious for being, well, a narcissist (though the word didn't exist yet). It was well known that the man was too consumed with his own beauty to find attraction in others. Echo found herself very attracted to Narcissus (most people were) but wasn't able to call out to him. Fortunately, he called out to his friends at that moment, asking, "Anyone here?" Echo, because of her curse, was only able to repeat the last word he spoke, "Here!" His calls and her responses continued, with Narcissus trying to determine who was actually there. Eventually the one-sided conversation allowed Echo to reveal herself to Narcissus. He asked whoever was there to join him, and Echo responded the same. She was convinced that he would feel for her what she felt for him. Excited, Echo ran up to Narcissus, taking his face in her hands. Narcissus was taken aback by this—he was shocked and not at all receptive to Echo's advances. He pushed her off him, forcefully telling her to go away.

Embarrassed and hurt, Echo ran from Narcissus and ended up in a nearby cave. There she stayed, her obsession with the man she'd seen from afar only growing as she withered and eventually died.

Narcissus found himself equally cursed. He was unable to love anyone but himself. In time, he found himself looking into a pool. There, he spotted a handsome man; he was quite taken with him. Narcissus immediately fell in love with the man staring back at him from the pool—i.e., his own reflection. He stared at his reflection, lounging on the banks of the pool, transfixed and unable to move, for so long that he, too, withered and died. In the place where he died, there was no body for his family to mourn; instead, there grew small yellow and gold flowers.

Now You Know

The ancient Greeks believed that Echo was (not surprisingly) where echoes come from. Her voice alone remains in caves around the world, only able to repeat the last word spoken by anyone nearby. Similarly, Narcissus is (also not surprisingly) where we get the word and concept *narcissism*, as well as the flower named for him, narcissus.

TYPHON and ECHIDNA

Two Primordial Monsters

AKA: Typhoeus (an older name) and Ekhidna (alternate spelling)

⌐⌐⌐⌐⌐⌐⌐

What's Their Deal?

Typhon and Echidna were two of the oldest monsters of Greek mythology. Typhon was born of Gaia and Tartarus, while Echidna was born of Ceto (an infamous sea monster) and Phorcys (a primordial sea god). Together, Typhon and Echidna spawned most of the most famous monstrous creatures of mythology.

There are many different descriptions of Typhon: Sometimes he's a storm monster, but he's most often snakelike in one way or another. A common description of him is that he had the top half of a man, and his bottom half was two snake tails. And, lest he seem too normal, his fingers were *one hundred snakes.* Typhon is also often described as having wings. Echidna's description is similar, though less horrifying: She had the top half of a woman, and her bottom half was a coiled snake.

The monstrous spawn of Typhon and Echidna include:

⋘ Cerberus, the three-headed dog who guarded the entrance to the Underworld.

- The many-headed Hydra (see Heracles's entry).

- The Chimera, a lion that breathed fire and had a goat's head protruding from its back and a snake for a tail (the Chimera was killed by the hero Bellerophon with the help of the famous flying horse Pegasus).

- The Crommyonian Sow, a fire-breathing pig killed by Theseus.

- The Caucasian Eagle, the eagle sent by Zeus to perpetually eat Prometheus's liver.

- The Hesperian Dragon, a dragon that guarded the Garden of the Hesperides.

- The Sphinx, a being that was part woman, part lion, and part eagle (see Oedipus's entry).

- The Nemean Lion (see Heracles's entry).

They were a very prolific couple!

The Story You Need to Know

The birth of Typhon is an example of the wrath of Gaia and what she's capable of when she's angry with her children or grand-children.

When Zeus had driven the Titans from their place as rulers over the world and defeated Kronos and all the Titans who'd sided with him in the Titanomachy, Gaia was *furious*. Her own grandson had defeated her children (his own parents)! Gaia wanted to punish Zeus, and to do this she gave birth to the most monstrous creature the world had seen: Typhon.

Typhon would have become powerful enough to take control of the whole earth had Zeus not defeated the monster before he

could reach his full potential. Zeus acted preemptively against him, sending reverberating thunder and lightning so strong that it shook the earth, the sea (it's said to have boiled!), the Underworld, and even Tartarus (an *even deeper* section of the Underworld), where the Titans were locked away. He sent so much lightning at Typhon that the monster was thrown off, shell-shocked. Zeus continued sending lightning, setting Typhon on fire and burning much of the earth around the creature as a result.

Their battle continued raging, getting more and more dramatic as it went on. The heat and fire caused by Zeus's lightning eventually became so intense that it *melted the earth*. Finally, though, Zeus was able to defeat Typhon for good, and he, too, was sent down to Tartarus with the defeated Titans.

According to some sources, Typhon wasn't imprisoned in Tartarus. Instead, it's said that he was trapped under the island of Sicily in Italy, where Mount Etna, an active volcano today, is evidence of Typhon's continued fury beneath the mountain.

Now You Know

There's a version of the battle between Zeus and Typhon in which Typhon actually manages to remove all Zeus's muscles from his body. In Roberto Calasso's beautiful novelization of Greek myths, *The Marriage of Cadmus and Harmony*, the hero Cadmus returns Zeus's sinews to his body.

PART 4

HEROES AND MORTALS

Mortals of Greek mythology, both hero and otherwise, played a vital role in the way the Greeks understood the natural world and the machinations of the gods. While not true of *every* story, many of the stories featuring mortals are examples of the ways in which the gods involved themselves in human lives, for better or worse (it was usually worse).

Many of the stories of women in this section detail those who were ruined in one way or another by Zeus. While the ancient Greeks loved Zeus and worshipped him, they also recognized that he and the other gods could do horrible things for little or no reason at all. This depiction was their way of understanding how humanity could do the same. There are also a number of stories about the hubris of humans—in other words, people who believed they were as capable, or more so, than the gods (these comparisons never went well for the humans). And then there are the heroes, (mostly) men who set out to kill monsters, complete quests, and save cities. Heroes were vital to the ancient Greek world. They were often associated with particular cities, and those cities worshipped them as though they were gods (and they were often the half-mortal children of gods).

Finally, there are the men of the Trojan War, who were written about in Homer's *Iliad* and *Odyssey*. These are two epic poems (novel-length poems) written sometime between 800 and 700 B.C.E. We don't actually know whether Homer existed—the works could have been compiled by many poets over many decades—but we do know that these works are an in-depth look into the ancient world in a way the other myths are not. The characters (Paris, Agamemnon, Achilles, and Odysseus) are in a category of their own because they originated not in folktales told regionally but in epic poems about specific stories that the ancient Greeks, by and large, believed were historical in nature. While they are categorized as heroes, they were not all heroic—you'll meet spoiled princes, a murderous warmonger, and a very flawed man in desperate search of his home.

SEMELE

A Princess of Thebes; Daughter of Cadmus and Harmonia

⌐⌐⌐⌐⌐⌐⌐

What's Her Deal?

Semele was a princess of the city of Thebes and a daughter of the city's founders, Cadmus and Harmonia. Semele was the first of the couple's descendants to suffer a tragic fate brought on by the curse placed upon the family (see Cadmus's entry for more on that curse). Semele's nephews Actaeon and Pentheus (see Dionysus's entry for more on Pentheus), along with the famous Oedipus are further examples of the curse on the family of Cadmus and Harmonia. Interestingly, Cadmus and Harmonia themselves weren't affected by the curse, save for knowing their children and grandchildren would be ruined by it.

Semele, as the mother of Dionysus, was one of the only mortal women to conceive a god upon having sex with Zeus (or any other Olympian!) and certainly the only mortal woman who mothered a god as powerful and important as Dionysus. A portion of the story of Zeus and Semele features in the Webtoon *Lore Olympus*.

The Story You Need to Know

Semele's story is another example of Zeus "falling in love" with a mortal or goddess. In this case Semele did love Zeus, and he seemed to love her too, in his own way. He was caring and promised her whatever she wanted. The two were together for a while before Semele became pregnant—they spent a number of nights together…enough to get to know each other (as much as was possible). Semele was aware who Zeus was, though she hadn't seen him in his true form.

It didn't really occur to Semele to question Zeus on his form until an old woman arrived to be a nurse to Semele. She and Semele spoke of the pregnancy and the father. Semele told her that it was the god Zeus himself! The old woman smiled, telling Semele that she hoped it really was Zeus, but that she'd heard of so many men convincing women that they were gods, only to abandon them when the child arrived. This was worrying, and Semele hadn't considered that could be possible. But it did seem too good to be true that the father of her new baby could be Zeus! She and the old woman continued talking about it, and eventually the woman convinced Semele to ask Zeus to show himself in his true form, the same way he appeared to his own wife, Hera, to prove to her that he was indeed Zeus, god of thunder and king of all the gods. It turns out, however, that the old woman convincing Semele of this was Hera herself: She intended to punish Zeus by punishing Semele.

The next time Semele saw Zeus, she did exactly as the old woman suggested. He tried to convince her against asking it of him, knowing that he'd promised her anything she wanted. So if she requested it, he would do it…but that could lead to her ruin. Semele assured Zeus that she did want him to show himself to her in the same way he showed himself to his own wife. Finally, Zeus agreed. He appeared to Semele in his true form. Thunder and lightning rained around them as Zeus transformed into his godly shape. In an instant, Semele was hit with a bolt of lightning and died immediately. Zeus had known this would happen, so he was prepared to take the unborn baby from her body. He sewed the baby into his thigh so the infant could continue incubating. Eventually the god Dionysus was born from Zeus's thigh. In time, Dionysus would take his place among the Olympians as the only Olympian with a mortal parent.

Dionysus being born of Zeus's thigh is sometimes used as an example of Zeus "giving birth" to another child himself. Like in Athena's case, though, the truth is that he caused the death of the child's mother and used his godly abilities to save him, even if he didn't save his mother.

Now You Know

The play *The Bacchae* by Euripides begins with Semele's own sisters still not believing that Zeus was the father of her child, even after her death at the hands of the god. The fact that, even after her death, they didn't believe Semele is another effect of the ongoing curse on their family (see Dionysus's entry for the story of that play).

IO

A Princess of Argos

⧉⧉⧉⧉⧉

What's Her Deal?

Io was a beautiful princess of Argos. She acted as a priestess at the temple of Hera (Argos is the city most beloved by the goddess Hera). Io would eventually become identified by some as the Egyptian goddess Isis. The proximity of various civilizations around the Mediterranean often led to gods and goddesses appearing in multiple cultures, serving as a way for people to see their own gods in foreign pantheons. In certain traditions, Io was associated with the moon.

A character named Io appears in the 2010 movie *Clash of the Titans*, and though she shares some similar characteristics with the original, she isn't explicitly *that* Io. In ancient popular culture, Io featured in the play *Prometheus Bound* by Aeschylus, in which her wanderings included her coming across the Titan Prometheus as he was bound in his perpetual punishment (see Prometheus's entry for this story).

The Story You Need to Know

Io's story begins like many other women's in Greek mythology: She was spotted by the king of the gods, Zeus. As a priestess of Hera (Zeus's wife), she spent much of her time worshipping the goddess in her temple. It was there that Zeus saw Io. It's said he "fell in love" with her. More likely, it was really yet another instance of Zeus forcing himself upon a woman. The encounter took place in the city of Argos, sacred to Hera, which added to the insult to her. Hera easily found out about Zeus's apparent affection for Io, and Zeus, realizing he was about to be caught with her, transformed Io into a cow in an effort to keep the truth hidden from his wife just a little while longer.

Hera was very familiar with her husband's methods of cover-up, so she understood immediately why Zeus was suddenly spending his time with a mysterious cow. In retribution, she made a point of asking Zeus for the cow as a gift, knowing he'd reveal his secret if he refused. So, Zeus gave Hera Io in the form of a cow, and, just as in the story of Semele, Hera used the opportunity to punish Io for what Zeus had done to her.

Hera assigned her beloved protector, a hundred-eyed giant named Argus Panoptes (*panoptes* means "all-eyed" or "all seeing"), to stand guard over Io and prevent Zeus from returning to her. Argus fastened Io the cow to an olive tree and watched over her day and night. With so many eyes, Argus never needed to close all of them at once, making him the perfect watchman. Zeus, though, was still very much infatuated with Io and sought to free her from Hera's grasp. He sent his son Hermes, the trickster god, down to earth to kill Argus and free Io. Hermes played music to lull Argus to sleep—a deep enough sleep that *all* his eyes were closed—and he slew the giant.

In her fury over the death of her beloved giant, Hera sent a gadfly to torment Io (who was still a cow). Io wandered all around the Greek mainland and the Mediterranean region as a whole, perpetually trying to get away from the fly, before eventually arriving in Egypt.

The all-seeing nature of Argus Panoptes is where Argus Filch, the Hogwarts caretaker in the Harry Potter series, gets his name. He somehow seems to always know what's going on in the castle, just like Argus Panoptes could see everything with all his eyes.

Now You Know

Io's wanderings led her all the way to Egypt, where, on the banks of the Nile, she finally found peace from the gadfly. The Greeks believed that her descendants ruled there for generations. This is how she became, according to some, identified with the Egyptian goddess Isis, who would have already been an established goddess of the region.

EUROPA

A Phoenician Princess

525252525

What's Her Deal?

Europa was a young woman from Phoenicia, an ancient civilization on the Mediterranean coast of the Middle East (in modern-day Lebanon and beyond). The Phoenicians were major trading partners with the ancient Greeks and eventually had colonial cities across the Middle East and northern Africa (the famous city of Carthage began as a Phoenician colony). Europa was a princess of the city of Tyre, the daughter of the king and queen and sister to Phoenix and Cadmus.

The Story You Need to Know

According to the early Alexandrian poet Moschus, Europa was awakened early one morning by a dream. In her dream she had seen two continents, both shaped like women, one near and one far, and both fighting for possession of her. One she knew was called Asia. Asia told Europa that she was her mother, and that

Asia was where she belonged. The other, whose name Europa didn't know, came at her more violently. That woman tried to drag Europa away, telling her that the king of the gods himself, Zeus, had decided Europa was to be possessed by the unnamed continent.

Europa awoke with a start, surprised and shaken by this dream. But she thought it was just that, a dream, and so she went about her day (the dream appears in writings by Moschus, but the rest of the story is more widely told). Together with some of her friends, Europa went down toward the seashore to pick flowers. To all the girls' surprise, they suddenly found themselves being approached by a large, stark-white bull. It seemed to come out of nowhere! The other girls were startled and backed away from the bull, but Europa was intrigued and found herself getting closer and closer to it. Eventually Europa was tempted to climb onto the bull's back. It let her climb on and didn't startle or move at all, so she wasn't worried. But as soon as Europa began riding the bull, it leapt, full speed, into the sea. Before any of Europa's friends could do anything about it, Europa was heading farther and farther out to sea. Europa panicked (how could she not?), but there wasn't anything she could do. Here she was, in the middle of the ocean, riding a strange bull!

Before long, the bull, with Europa still on its back, arrived on an island. It waded to shore, and Europa immediately jumped off, trying to regain her composure after such a startling (and, frankly, weird) experience. She turned back to look at the bull, but it wasn't there. Or, it was, but it wasn't a bull anymore: The white bull had transformed into the god Zeus. Zeus told her that this island was hers now, and that here she would give birth to a son who would be king of the island and the first of a dynasty of kings. The island was Crete, and the kingdom was founded in the city they called Knossos (see the stories of Pasiphaë and Minos, Theseus, Ariadne and Phaedra, and the Minotaur for more on the epic stories from Knossos, Crete).

Before Zeus left Europa alone on the island, he assaulted her and impregnated her with the child who would be named Minos, the first king of Crete and the mythical founder of the Minoan civilization. The two went on to have more children, including Rhadamanthys and Sarpedon, both famous in their own right.

A silver lining…the story of Europa is one of the few examples of Zeus's acts of adultery that doesn't result in horrible punishment by Hera! Though she was far from her home, Europa did find some level of happiness with her children on Crete.

Now You Know

As you might imagine, the continent of Europe is said to be named for Europa. It was the continent of her dreams that tried to drag her off with the blessing of Zeus. It's not a particularly nice story for how Europe got its name, but it is the first of *many* dramatic stories of bulls and the island of Crete.

LEDA

A Queen of Sparta; Mother of Castor, Polydeuces, Helen, and Clytemnestra

᠎᠎᠎᠎᠎

What's Her Deal?

Leda was a queen of Sparta, married to the king Tyndareus, and mother of the twins Castor and Polydeuces, as well as Helen and Clytemnestra. She is best known for featuring in various works of art with Zeus, who appears in the form of a swan. Appearing as a swan in order to be with a woman is one of the more *creative* ways in which Zeus impregnated a mortal with famously divine children. It is usually easy to identify Leda in ancient imagery because of this unique situation.

The Story You Need to Know

The story of Leda's fate is yet another tale of Zeus taking an interest in a mortal woman and appearing as a creature other than human in order to assault her (and there are many more instances that didn't even make it into this book!). As a swan,

Zeus assaulted the queen of Sparta, and she became pregnant. However, on the very same night that Zeus was with Leda, she was also with her own husband, Tyndareus. Because of this (and a lack of understanding of the physical limitations of a woman's body!), Leda became pregnant by both men simultaneously. When the time came, Leda gave birth to a total of *four* children in the form of *two* eggs, which she laid as though she herself were the swan.

Leda laid two eggs, from which hatched the twins Castor and Polydeuces (who is more famously known by his Roman/Latin name, Pollux), and Helen (yes, *that* Helen) and Clytemnestra. Two of the children were fathered by Zeus, and two were fathered by Tyndareus, making two mortal and two divine, though it's not always clear which is which. Depending on the source, sometimes the twins each come from a different egg!

Castor and Polydeuces went on to partake in a number of heroic quests, including accompanying Jason and the other Argonauts on the search for the Golden Fleece, the famed Calydonian Boar Hunt (see Atalanta's entry), and rescuing their sister Helen when she, *as a child*, was kidnapped by Theseus. The twins waged war on the entire city of Athens to save Helen and succeeded in having her returned to her home. While Polydeuces was always considered a son of Zeus, both twins were ultimately deified after their deaths for their lifetime of heroism and valor. They were devoted brothers throughout their lives and were never rivals of each other. As deities, Castor and Polydeuces were worshipped as the gods of horsemanship and protectors of sailors and travelers, among other more specific attributes.

Together, Castor and Polydeuces were known as the Dioscuri (from the Greek *Dioskouroi*) and were eventually placed in the sky as the constellation Gemini, the twins. The pair died and were made into gods before the Trojan War began and so didn't partake in that more famous war waged over the ownership of their sister.

Once she was old enough, Clytemnestra married Agamemnon, the king of Mycenae. A short while later, Helen married Agamemnon's brother, Menelaus, who, as her husband, took the title of king of Sparta. Helen and Clytemnestra would go on to become embroiled in the Trojan War each in their own way. Helen's kidnapping by the Trojan prince Paris brought the two regions to war when Menelaus sought to bring her back with the help of his brother. While the men were away at war, Clytemnestra remained home in Mycenae, plotting her husband's murder for the next ten years (Agamemnon had sacrificed their daughter for a bit of good wind!—see the entry on Clytemnestra and Her Children for more on Agamemnon's murder).

Now You Know

There are many variations when it comes to which children of Leda were fathered by Zeus and which by her husband, Tyndareus. The same goes for who was born of an egg, or which children were born together in which egg. It's typically understood that, while Castor and Polydeuces were twins, it was Helen and Polydeuces who were born divine.

ACTAEON

A Shepherd and Hunter of Boeotia

What's His Deal?

Actaeon, born to Autonoë and Aristaeus in the region of Boeotia, was a young man and skilled hunter. He was a descendant of Cadmus and Harmonia, the founders of Thebes and parents of Autonoë. This relationship meant that Actaeon's fate was a result of the curse on that family (see the entries on Cadmus, Semele, Oedipus, and Dionysus). The family of Cadmus and Harmonia saw *a lot* of tragedy.

The Story You Need to Know

The story of Actaeon is told most beautifully (and *viscerally*) by the Roman poet Ovid. Actaeon and his friends and their dogs were out hunting in the forests of Boeotia. They'd had a very successful day and had killed an excessive number of animals. The group took a break during the hottest part of the afternoon; they were tired from all the killing and wanted to relax a little. Actaeon wandered off from the group to explore the forest.

Meanwhile, the notoriously virginal goddess Artemis was also out in the forests of Boeotia that day—and she, too, was tired and seeking a break from the heat. Artemis and her nymphs went to her special cave with a small pool to cool off. There they took off their clothes and began to bathe one another in the pool. Just as they had begun, Actaeon came upon them. He had managed to find the cave in the depths of the forest, and then the pool within the cave. Before the nymphs could stop him, Actaeon had seen them and the goddess Artemis naked and bathing.

Witnessing Artemis's unclothed body, whether intentionally or not, was one of the worst things a man could do. She proudly avoided men and had no desire to have them see her in anything less than her full hunting gear. The nymphs crowded around her, trying to hide the goddess from Actaeon's view, but it was too late: He'd seen all of her.

Once she had gotten over the initial embarrassment, Artemis flew into a fury. She cursed Actaeon, causing him to transform into a stag. Antlers grew from his head, and his body slowly lengthened and grew fur until he was no longer human. Once transformed, Actaeon fled through the forests and eventually neared his friends and their pack of hunting dogs. The friends called out for Actaeon, wondering where he'd gone, and the stag approached them. His friends saw the stag and had no idea the animal was actually their friend—they saw only another stag to hunt. Keen to keep the hunt going, Actaeon's friends set the dogs on the stag, and they viciously ripped Actaeon the stag apart.

Now You Know

The family of Cadmus and Harmonia saw a whole lot of tragedy, but the couple themselves experienced none of that. Nothing particularly bad happened to them, but their children and grandchildren (and even further ancestors down the line) suffered some of the most tragic fates in Greek mythology. Actaeon is one of the most famous examples.

THESEUS

A Hero and Prince of Athens

52525252

What's His Deal?

Theseus was a hero and considered to be one of the first kings of Athens (but first, he was a prince of Athens). The Athenians thought of him as their founder and worshipped him for it. You may know the name Theseus from the movie *Immortals*, though that portrayal of Theseus doesn't resemble the actual myth.

Theseus was the son of Aegeus, though possibly also the son of Poseidon. Aegeus had been trying to have a child—he was the king of Athens and needed an heir—but the two women he'd married already hadn't been able to get pregnant by him. Finally, he went to the Oracle and eventually ended up in the city of Troezen, where he slept with his friend's daughter, Aethra (who was also with Poseidon on the same night, hence the confusion). Aegeus returned to Athens, leaving Aethra in Troezen, where she eventually gave birth to a son: Theseus.

The Story You Need to Know

There are a number of stories associated with Theseus, as with many of the heroes, but the most famous tells of his journey to Crete. Before Theseus returned to Athens and claimed his place as the son of the king Aegeus and, therefore, the heir to the throne of Athens, the city had gotten itself into some trouble with Crete. Minos had waged war against Athens, and Athens was losing. Instead of being destroyed completely, the two cities agreed to a deal: Every seven years, Athens would send a group of young men and women to Crete to be sacrificed to the Minotaur in the Labyrinth (see the entries on Pasiphaë and Minos and on the Minotaur for their origin stories).

Theseus wanted to put a stop to this, to save Athens from having to sacrifice any more of its young people. So, Theseus volunteered to be one of the young men next sacrificed. Aegeus was worried that his son wouldn't survive, so before he left, he had Theseus promise that when his ship returned to Athens, he would change the color of its sails from black to white if he survived killing the Minotaur. That way, when Aegeus was watching from the cliffs, waiting for his son's return, he would see the white sails from afar and immediately know that Theseus was alive and well (what a relief that would be!). Theseus made this promise to his father and set out for Crete.

When Theseus arrived in Knossos, on the island of Crete, he met Ariadne, a princess and the daughter of Pasiphaë and Minos. Theseus seduced Ariadne—she was young and believed she'd fallen in love with this handsome Athenian prince (Theseus had a *very* bad track record with women). Wanting to help the man she believed she loved, Ariadne gave Theseus thread and told him all she knew about getting through the Labyrinth. Theseus used the thread to track his movements in the maze; that way he could follow it to get back out. He reached the Minotaur and slew the monster. Because of Ariadne, Theseus was able to kill the Minotaur and escape the Labyrinth and Crete itself. Ariadne joined Theseus and the young Athenians as they sailed off from Crete.

Meanwhile, Aegeus was waiting for his son's return, worried sick that Theseus wouldn't survive. Every day, he stood on the cliffs watching for those white sails on the horizon, proof that his son had survived and would soon be home safe. Finally, sails appeared…but they weren't white. Aegeus could see in the distance the very same black sails that Theseus had left with. His heart was broken—Aegeus understood this to mean that Theseus had died trying to kill the Minotaur, and the ship was sailing back without him. In his grief, Aegeus threw himself off the cliffs and into the sea below. That sea took Aegeus's name (the Aegean Sea).

A short while later, Theseus returned home safely. He'd simply forgotten to change his sails.

Now You Know

While Theseus was traveling to Athens from Troezen, planning to reunite with his father, he encountered "bandits." By the time he reached Athens, he had a number of murders under his belt: Theseus had killed men who, allegedly, were murderers themselves. Theseus always made a point of killing them in the same way that they were said to have murdered others. This included bending two trees and tying a man's feet to one, his arms to the other, and then letting the trees straighten, resulting in the man being ripped in half.

Hippolyta

An Amazonian Queen

AKA: Hippolyte (alternate spelling)

———◆———

While most sources agree that Theseus *definitely* encountered an Amazonian queen, there is no consensus on which Amazonian queen Theseus met—it was either Hippolyta or Antiope (or possibly another woman entirely!). For the sake of clarity, we will refer to the Amazonian queen in question as Hippolyta.

Theseus traveled to the land of the Amazons with his friend Pirithous, the same friend who helped Theseus kidnap the famous Helen of Sparta—later of Troy (see Leda's entry)—and attempt to kidnap Persephone, the queen of the Underworld herself. For this, he and Pirithous were trapped in the Underworld until they were saved by Heracles. Theseus and Pirithous were the type of friends who just *had* to get into trouble together.

When they sailed to the land of the Amazons (often called Themiscyra), they were welcomed by the women. The Amazons weren't afraid of men; they knew their strengths and instead welcomed them as guests of their city. Theseus took advantage of this: Hippolyta, their queen, brought welcome gifts to Theseus at his ship, and after she boarded the ship to bestow these generous gifts to the visitors, Theseus set sail, kidnapping the queen. Theseus assaulted Hippolyta, and she became pregnant with a son, Hippolytus.

> Although there is very little written about the mythological Amazons, their existence was based on a civilization (or multiple civilizations) of real warrior women who regularly tangled with the ancient Greeks.

Another story of Hippolyta has her ultimate fate lying with the hero Heracles. One of Heracles's famed Twelve Labors was to retrieve Hippolyta's war belt. The war belt was given to her by Ares himself, and she wore it with pride until Heracles arrived, seeking it. Just as with Theseus, Hippolyta didn't fear Heracles and so welcomed him, offering him the war belt as a gift. Hera, though, was present throughout the labors of Heracles, causing trouble in whatever way she could. She convinced the other Amazons that Heracles was trying to kidnap their queen, so they attempted to save her. Heracles, seeing the women coming at him in that way, ignored how nice and welcoming Hippolyta had been, and he killed her. He was able to fend off the rest of the Amazons and sailed away with the war belt that Hippolyta had given him kindly and willingly. Most of the ancient Greek heroes lacked the more compassionate aspects of true heroism.

Hippolyta and the Amazons are some of the most famous mythological women, yet there is very little recorded information about them. The Amazonomachy (the war with the Amazons) was depicted on the west metopes of the Parthenon in Athens, copies of which appear in the Acropolis Museum. The Amazons and their home of Themiscyra feature in the long-running comic series *Wonder Woman*. More recently, Hippolyta and Antiope were portrayed in the 2017 DC movie *Wonder Woman* as Diana's aunt and mother, respectively.

Ariadne and Phaedra

Princesses of Crete; Goddess and Wife of Dionysus; Wife of Theseus

AKA: Libera (Roman/Latin of Ariadne)

Ariadne and Phaedra were the daughters of Pasiphaë and Minos, princesses of Crete and sisters to, among others, the Minotaur (to him, they were only half sisters). When Theseus arrived on Crete to kill the Minotaur, Ariadne fell for him. He was handsome and exciting—a prince from faraway Athens who needed her help. She helped him, and only with her aid was Theseus able to kill the Minotaur. Without her there to provide the thread that guided his way, and possibly even the sword with which he killed the monster, Theseus would never have made it through.

Once Theseus had killed the Minotaur, Ariadne further helped him escape the island itself, and together they landed on the island of Naxos. There, while Ariadne was sleeping, Theseus abandoned her (he did so, so many awful things!). Ariadne awoke on a strange island, having helped a strange man kill her half brother and defy her kingdom, having left her entire family behind for this man…suddenly *alone*. She was horrified with what Theseus had done and where she now found herself. But almost as quickly as Theseus had given her up, she was saved when the god Dionysus arrived on the island with a group of his Maenads. Dionysus, the god of wine and revelry, fell in love with Ariadne, and she with him. They quickly married and had children, and eventually Ariadne was deified and lived with Dionysus on Mount Olympus.

After Theseus abandoned Ariadne on the island of Naxos, he went on to marry her sister, Phaedra. According to some, this occurred much later in his life, making it just a bit less offensive. While he was married to Phaedra, the couple visited the city where Theseus had grown up, Troezen. There he met his son, Hippolytus. His son by the Amazonian queen Hippolyta had been sent to Troezen as a child, where he grew into an impressive young man. He was a good athlete and good-looking, and he chose to worship the goddess Artemis over the goddess Aphrodite.

Hippolytus's choice of Artemis over Aphrodite led Aphrodite to curse him. The curse, though, affected Theseus's wife more than it affected Hippolytus himself. In Troezen, Hippolytus caught the eye of Phaedra. Phaedra found herself falling in love with Hippolytus, and she acted on it, confessing her love. Hippolytus, aside from also being her *stepson*, wasn't interested in love or women. He rejected Phaedra, and her cursed love for him drove her to kill herself. Theseus, finding Phaedra's suicide note, confronted Hippolytus and banished him from Troezen. This story is told in *Hippolytus*, one of the ancient playwright Euripides's more famous tragic plays.

HERACLES

A Hero of Thebes; Son of Zeus

AKA: Hercules (Roman/Latin)

᠊᠊᠊᠊᠊᠊᠊᠊

What's His Deal?

Heracles, better known by his Roman/Latin name, Hercules, was a hero of ancient Greece. He was one of the most famous heroes of mythology and has, by far, the most stories associated with him. Heracles was later taken on by the Romans as one of their most important heroes, which is where the widespread use of the name Hercules comes from. While his Greek name is older and more original (the Greek Heracles was said to have sacked Troy long before even the Trojan War!), he is rarely referred to by that name beyond the Greek sources. Heracles was the son of Zeus and a mortal woman named Alcmene and was, by far, the strongest, most impressive of the heroes. There are numerous instances of Hera punishing those involved with Zeus, but the case of Heracles is legendary. Most of the trials he faced were a direct result of Hera's attempts to destroy him for simply being the son of Zeus— she put much more effort into punishing Heracles than she did with any of Zeus's many other forays outside their marriage.

Heracles (or Hercules) is well known in popular culture. He is a character in a Disney movie and TV series, both called *Hercules* (a much more entertaining viewing once you know the truth about Heracles and Hera!), as well as the 1995 live-action TV show *Hercules: The Legendary Journeys*. In more recent years, two movies featured the hero: *Hercules* (2014) and *The Legend of Hercules* (also from 2014; it was a big year for Herc). This is only a short list of his credits. Hercules (though, really, Heracles) has been featured in more movies and TV shows than any other Greek hero.

The Story You Need to Know

While Heracles partook in any number of heroic quests and battles (he helped the Olympian gods defeat the giants in the Gigantomachy; he saved Theseus from his imprisonment in the Underworld; he sacked Troy a generation before the Trojan War), he is most famous for the Twelve Labors he completed for the king Eurystheus. The labors came about from a tragedy: Heracles was married to a woman named Megara (where Disney's *Hercules* got the name Meg!), and they had three children. Hera, however, drove him mad, and he killed them all. Once it was done, his madness faded away, and he was left with the guilt of his actions. He sought guidance from the Oracle of Delphi, who told him he needed to seek purification from King Eurystheus of Mycenae. Eurystheus was driven by Hera, who was forever punishing Heracles for being the son of her husband. So, Eurystheus assigned to Heracles Twelve Labors, each one impossible for most other heroes:

- The First Labor: Heracles was sent to kill the Nemean Lion (see Typhon and Echidna's entry), which couldn't be pierced by any weapons. Fortunately, Heracles's strength allowed him to choke the lion rather than pierce it.

- The Second Labor: He had to kill the Lernean Hydra, a many-headed monstrosity who grew two heads every time one was removed! Every time Heracles cut off one of the heads, two more grew in its place. Eventually Heracles was able to cauterize each neck when the head was removed, preventing regrowth.

- The Third Labor: Heracles was sent to bring back a stag with antlers of gold, sacred to Artemis. This took him a whole year (!), but he managed to finally succeed.

- The Fourth Labor: Heracles was sent to capture the Erymanthian Boar, a monstrous boar terrorizing the region. Heracles trapped it.

- The Fifth Labor: Heracles was forced to clean the Augean Stables in a day (a very different sort of labor). These stables hadn't been cleaned in *ages*, and Heracles had to divert a couple of rivers and flood them out in order to clean them.

- The Sixth Labor: Heracles drove away the Stymphalian Birds, a flock of birds causing great trouble. Athena helped him with this task.

- The Seventh Labor: He had to capture the Cretan Bull (see the entry on Pasiphaë and Minos). He succeeded and released it in Marathon, where it became known as the Marathonian Bull, which was later captured by Theseus.

- The Eighth Labor: Heracles had to capture the man-eating horses of Diomedes. This was easy; he killed Diomedes and captured the horses.

- The Ninth Labor: Heracles was told to bring back the war-belt of Hippolyta, queen of the Amazons.

- The Tenth Labor: Heracles captured the Cattle of Geryon (a monster with three bodies!).

- The Eleventh Labor: This was a tricky one. Heracles had to bring Eurystheus golden apples of the Hesperides... but he didn't know where to find them. Heracles traveled and eventually found the Titan Atlas (he famously held the *heavens* on his shoulders, though art would suggest the earth itself), the father of the Hesperides, who helped Heracles obtain the apples.

- The Twelfth (and Final!) Labor: Heracles had to retrieve Cerberus from the Underworld, where he also saved Theseus.

Even after Heracles had completed the Twelve Labors, he was unable to rest or be at peace. He spent the rest of his life completing a host of other feats of heroism before, upon his death, he was made into a god and brought to Mount Olympus, where he married Hebe, the goddess of youth and the daughter of Hera and Zeus.

Now You Know

When Heracles brought back the Cattle of Geryon, he had to travel a great distance. Once he succeeded, he set up a monument to his travels all the way there: These are the Pillars of Hercules, at the Strait of Gibraltar. Alternately, he built the Pillars to help Atlas hold the heavens!

PERSEUS

A Hero; Son of Zeus

᠎᠎᠎᠎᠎᠎᠎ 5252525252 ᠎᠎᠎᠎᠎᠎᠎

What's His Deal?

Perseus was a famous hero of Greek mythology. He appears in many pop culture representations of mythology, but they usually neglect to mention one wild thing: Perseus was conceived in one of the most incredible and entertaining incidents of all Greek mythology. Zeus came to Perseus's mother, Danaë, as, get this, a *shower of gold*. That's all it took, and she became pregnant with Perseus.

Danaë was imprisoned by her father, Acrisius. The Oracle told Acrisius that Danaë's son would overthrow him, so he locked her up to try to prevent this prophecy from happening. But Zeus (the perpetual troublemaker) felt he simply *had to* be with Danaë (it's unlikely she felt the same way), so he appeared to her as the aforementioned shower of gold.

Perseus and his mother eventually escaped Acrisius, but this did not solve their problems. They then found themselves in a kingdom ruled by Polydectes, a man who wanted to marry Danaë. Polydectes was even more troubling than Zeus (though far less entertaining; he didn't appear as a shower of gold!). Fortunately for storytelling purposes, Polydectes's attempts to have Perseus killed so that he could be with Danaë resulted in some heroic adventures for Perseus.

You may know Perseus from *Clash of the Titans*, the original or the remake, or from the Percy Jackson book series, in which a version of young Perseus is the main character (though with Poseidon as his father instead of Zeus).

The Story You Need to Know

Polydectes wanted to marry Danaë, but her son, Perseus, saw through his deceit and worked to convince his mother against it. In an attempt to kill Perseus and rid himself of this obstacle, Polydectes sent Perseus to bring back the head of the Gorgon Medusa (the Gorgons were three mysterious, somewhat monstrous, sisters). This would not be an easy quest: Not only was Medusa hiding far away from prying human eyes; she also had snakes for hair and turned men to stone with a single glance. Polydectes was sure Perseus would die, leaving him free to marry Danaë.

Thankfully for Perseus, Athena was there to lend him a helping hand (she usually was, when it came to heroes). She provided him with all he would need to find Medusa and bring back her head. She gave him instructions on where exactly to go: First, he would pay a visit to the Graeae, three old and very haggard women who shared one eye and one tooth between them, because they knew how to get to the Garden of the Hesperides, where there were weapons he could use to defeat Medusa. The Graeae were wary of helping Perseus, so he held their eye and tooth hostage until they gave up the location of the Hesperides.

When he reached the garden where the golden apples grew, he was given the weapons: a bag in which he could keep Medusa's head, a sword from Zeus, and a shield from Athena. When he reached Medusa, he was able to use the shield as a mirror, keeping track of her without looking her in the eye, and he quite easily removed the poor (if monstrous) woman's head to bring back to Polydectes. However, once Perseus had cut off Medusa's head, from her severed neck sprang a young man named Chrysaor and the famous flying horse himself, Pegasus. Contrary to much popular culture, Perseus never had the chance to ride Pegasus, though he was fortunate enough to witness the horse's birth.

Pegasus is *one* flying horse *named* Pegasus. Flying horses in general are not referred to as *pegasus* or *pegasi*. There is more than one flying horse in Greek mythology, but only one is called Pegasus.

On his way back to Polydectes, Perseus stopped in Aethiopia in Africa, where he met the princess Andromeda. Andromeda was to be sacrificed to a sea monster (it *was not* a Kraken, that's Norse mythology) in penance for her mother, Cassiopeia, bragging that Andromeda was more beautiful than a goddess. (This is an ongoing theme in Greek mythology. One must not *ever* compare themselves or anyone else favorably to a god.) Perseus found the woman chained to a rock awaiting the monster. He did away with its head just as he had Medusa's and married the newly freed Andromeda.

Together, Perseus and Andromeda traveled back to Polydectes, where Perseus presented the man with Medusa's head. As planned, this reveal transformed Polydectes to stone and freed Perseus and his mother, Danaë, from Polydectes's influence.

Now You Know

While Pegasus is known for being ridden by Hercules in Disney's film of the same name, and by Perseus in *Clash of the Titans*, he was truly only ever ridden by the hero Bellerophon. Together, the pair famously slew the Chimera, a monstrous lion with a goat's head growing off its back and a snake for a tail.

Medusa

A Gorgon

AKA: Medousa (alternate spelling)

———◆———

Medusa was one of three Gorgon sisters. The other two were named Stheno and Euryale. All three were daughters of the sea monster Ceto and the sea god Phorcys, but only Medusa was mortal. According to much early Greek mythology, Medusa was a monster born of monsters, but this isn't always the case, and later, into Roman times, her story developed and changed. The sisters were often described as winged monsters, covered in snakes, with enormous, gnashing teeth, who lived near the equally monstrous Graeae, also daughters of Phorcys.

According to later mythology, Medusa was a very different character. She was still most famous for her snakes-for-hair and for turning men to stone with one look, but she was depicted as much more woman than monster. In the later, more detailed interpretations of Medusa, these traits were instead curses placed upon her. As told by the Roman poet Ovid in one of the most tragic stories in classical mythology, Medusa was once a beautiful priestess of Athena, famous for her luxuriant hair. One day she was in Athena's temple, worshipping the goddess, when the god Poseidon came upon her, transfixed. Like his brother Zeus, Poseidon had a habit of taking whatever woman he wanted, so he assaulted Medusa. Athena, being a virgin goddess, was deeply offended by this act that took place in her temple, of all places.

Since she couldn't punish Poseidon, a god older and more powerful than herself, she punished Medusa. Athena transformed Medusa's beautiful hair into horrible snakes and caused the woman to turn men to stone with just a look. In this version, Perseus's quest to kill Medusa is a much sadder story. He wasn't there to kill a dangerous monster but rather a woman who was the victim of a god's actions. Chrysaor and Pegasus, the children birthed from Medusa's death, were children of Poseidon's assault, Poseidon being the god of horses. After Perseus used Medusa's head as a weapon, it was placed in Athena's shield, where it appears in most visual representations of the goddess.

Some interpret the act by Athena not as a punishment but instead as a means of preventing further trauma to Medusa. After Athena's changes, Medusa was no longer appealing to predatory men or gods, and she also had the ability to defend herself: She could turn them into stone. In either case, Ovid's stunning version of her story is much more sympathetic than most other representations. While this sympathetic version of Medusa is most commonly ascribed to Ovid alone, even the early Greek writer Hesiod explains that Medusa was assaulted by the god Poseidon, making this detail one of the most ancient interpretations of her story.

The image of a Gorgon, specifically the head of Medusa, was used as protection in ancient Greece and Rome. This imagery was and is especially important in Sicily, where a Gorgon is part of the region's official flag.

JASON

A Hero and Prince of Iolchus

AKA: Iason (alternate spelling)

525252525252

What's His Deal?

Jason was a hero best known for his ship, his quest, and the woman he married. He was the captain of the *Argo*, the ship that the group called the Argonauts took on the quest for the Golden Fleece. The Argonauts included the heroine Atalanta, the twins Castor and Polydeuces (see Leda's entry), Orpheus (see his and Eurydice's entry), Theseus, and even Heracles himself. These heroes are more well known than Jason, but perhaps even more famous was his wife, the witch Medea. The story of Jason, Medea, and the Argonauts is featured in a 1963 movie called *Jason and the Argonauts*, which is perhaps best remembered for its stop-motion skeletons.

Mythologically, Jason was rightfully a prince of Iolchus, but his father was removed from the throne by his brother and Jason's uncle, Pelias. As a child, Jason had been hidden away, only to return as an adult and missing a sandal. A one-sandaled man had been foretold to Pelias as causing his ruin, so Pelias was wary of Jason's return and immediately sought to have him killed by sending him on a quest to bring back the famed Golden Fleece, a sheep with fur of literal gold.

The Story You Need to Know

The usurper king of Iolchus, Pelias, assigned to Jason the task of retrieving the famed Golden Fleece from the far-off region of Colchis (site of modern-day Georgia, the country on the Black Sea). Jason was eager to have a heroic task to complete and, though Pelias knew it to be nearly impossible to achieve, accepted the quest. He put the call out all around Greece, seeking the bravest heroes to sail with him. Famous heroes came from all around, and the group set sail for the east.

First, they stopped on the island of Lemnos, where they encountered a city of only women. They quickly learned that the Lemnian women had rebelled against the men of the island and had killed every one. Now they were living peacefully with no men in sight. Though the Argonauts were a little afraid of these women, they were welcomed and enjoyed a good meal and a nice place to rest before they continued on. When they next reached land, they lost Heracles and his beloved friend and lover, Hylas, who was taken by nymphs. Heracles couldn't stop searching for Hylas, so the Argonauts went on without him.

Jason and the Argonauts encountered many other monsters and upsets en route before finally reaching Colchis, where they hoped to find the Golden Fleece. There, they spoke to the king, Aeëtes, who introduced them to his daughter, Medea, before asking why they were there. Aeëtes was furious to hear what they were after, though he couldn't show it, as he had already welcomed them as guests. Instead, he assigned Jason further impossible tasks in an effort to kill him indirectly.

> The ancient concept of *xenia* was something the Greeks took very seriously. This was the guest-host relationship, and it was sacred. If you hosted someone, or if you were a guest of someone, neither could be harmed, lest you risk some horrible punishment from the gods.

Aeëtes put Jason through a host of trials that should have killed him but didn't, because he had help. A spell had been placed upon Aeëtes's daughter, Medea, and she fell in love with Jason and did all she could to help him. With the help of Medea (via her magic and her intellect), Jason completed every trial Aeëtes assigned to him, each one more dangerous than the last.

Finally, once more with the vital aid of Medea, Jason and the Argonauts were able to steal the Golden Fleece from Aeëtes and escape from Colchis, bringing Medea with them. She also brought her brother, Apsyrtus, but she had a purpose for him. When her father began pursuing the *Argo* in his own ship, Medea sought to distract him. She killed her brother on board the *Argo*, in full view of her father, and slowly, deliberately cut her brother into as many pieces as she could, one by one flinging the pieces into the sea. Aeëtes, seeing this, was forced to stop and collect all the pieces of his son, thus delaying him long enough for the *Argo* to escape. The remaining story of Jason and Medea is covered in Medea's entry.

Now You Know

While Jason is a famous hero, there isn't much heroism that can actually be attributed to him. Without the Argonauts, he wouldn't have made it to Colchis, and without Medea, there is no way he would have survived Aeëtes's tasks, let alone returned to Iolchus with the Golden Fleece.

MEDEA

A Witch; Daughter of Aeëtes; Granddaughter of the Titan Helios

᠉᠉᠉᠉᠉

What's Her Deal?

Medea was the daughter of Aeëtes, who was the son of the Titan Helios and brother to Circe. It's never really clear who her mother was, though according to at least one source, it could have been the witch Hecate. Regardless of who her mother was, she came from a magical, witchy family. Medea grew up in Colchis, in the kingdom where Aeëtes was a tyrant.

Medea is most famous for the play named for her, written by the ancient Greek tragedian Euripides (though many other ancient playwrights and poets wrote about her too). The play is still performed in various iterations today. Her name has become synonymous with losing one's mind and committing murder, but her story isn't as simple as that. Medea is one of the most complex characters in Greek mythology, and the depiction of her in Euripides's play is an example of a truly fascinating, flawed, and sympathetic woman in a world dominated by stories of men.

The Story You Need to Know

After their escape from Aeëtes in Colchis and the murder of Medea's brother, Apsyrtus, Medea and Jason eventually returned to his home city of Iolchus (see Jason's entry for the story). There, they met with Pelias, the king who had sent Jason on the quest for the Golden Fleece, and who had since forced Jason's father to kill himself.

Jason was heartbroken and furious, but he knew who would be able to help. Medea had solved every problem he'd ever had to face, so surely she could make this right (Jason would have been *nothing* without Medea). Medea had the perfect plan. She offered to use her magic on Pelias, telling his daughters that she could make their father young and healthy through a certain ritual. They jumped at the idea: That would be amazing! But instead of making Pelias younger, Medea caused his daughters to kill their own father in a bloody and violent ritual. This was, perhaps, more vicious than Jason had imagined, but it worked! After the killing, though, the two were forced to flee Iolchus. They arrived next in the city of Corinth.

Medea and Jason lived in Corinth for many years, presumably happy enough. In that time, they had two sons who grew to be young children before Jason decided he'd grown bored of Medea. Jason announced that he intended to marry a Greek princess in order to give himself more importance and power in the Greek world. This would ruin Medea, because there was no divorce—instead, she would be abandoned and forced to seek charity in order to keep herself and her children alive.

In her horrified fury, Medea threatened the life of the Corinthian princess Jason intended to marry. The threat was heard by the princess's father, the king, who threatened to exile Medea. Exile was a fate even worse than what Jason was already inflicting upon her (women had no power without a husband or father—a woman living in exile had *nothing*).

This was the final straw for Medea. She thought about everything she'd given Jason—she'd abandoned her family and killed people for him, even her brother. None of that seemed to mean anything to him; he thought only of himself. So, Medea pretended to be very sorry for what she'd said and begged for a second chance. She sent their children to see their new stepmother to convince her that Medea deserved to stay in Corinth. She sent along a tiara and a robe as gifts for the princess. The gifts set the princess on fire and melted her skin. When her father rushed to save her, they melted his skin too. Jason's new bride and new father-in-law were dead.

When Jason reached Medea, horrified and furious with her for what she'd done, she told him that she'd killed their children too. Facing such a bleak future, they probably would have starved, so she prevented such a fate by instead taking their lives.

Now You Know

Because Medea came from Colchis, she was considered to be a foreigner, a non-Greek. Xenophobia existed in the ancient world too, and the Greeks were often wary of those who came from elsewhere and whose native language wasn't Greek. This was a large part of why Medea was treated so poorly by Jason and by the Corinthians (if she'd been Greek, he couldn't have just left her, ruined, because they would have been legally married).

CADMUS

A Hero; Founder of Thebes; a Prince of the Phoenicians

AKA: Kadmos (alternate spelling)

ᒧᒣᒪᒣᒪᒣᒪᒣ

What's His Deal?

Cadmus was a prince of Tyre, a city of the Phoenicians. He was the brother of Europa, the young woman Zeus kidnapped in the form of a bull. Cadmus and his wife, Harmonia, went on to found the ancient Greek city of Thebes. His descendants are called the Cadmeians and exist throughout many of the most famous stories from Greek mythology (see entries on Semele, Dionysus, Actaeon, and Oedipus).

Cadmus and Harmonia rarely, if ever, feature into pop culture—however, there is a beautiful novelization of Greek myths by Roberto Calasso that is named for the couple, *The Marriage of Cadmus and Harmony*.

The Story You Need to Know

When Cadmus's sister, Europa, was kidnapped by Zeus, Cadmus took it upon himself to find her and bring her back to her home in Phoenicia. Cadmus was smart, and he knew there was no use in wandering the region aimlessly, hoping to stumble upon his sister. So he visited the Oracle of Delphi for guidance on how to find her. But the Oracle told him that he needn't bother; his sister had been taken by Zeus, and because of that there was no use in trying. He wouldn't be able to bring her back even if he could find her. Instead, Cadmus was told his fate lay in the founding of a great city on the Greek mainland, in Boeotia. The Oracle went on to tell him that in order to locate the spot on which he was meant to found the city, he would find a cow shortly after leaving Delphi. He was to follow that cow to where it lay down, and there he would found his city.

Cadmus followed the Oracle's instructions, and eventually the cow lay down in what would become the ancient city of Thebes (it's said that Cadmus named the city in honor of the Egyptian city of the same name). There, Cadmus encountered the Ismenian dragon, a monstrous creature named for the spring it guarded. Cadmus slew the dragon and, upon the guidance of Athena (who quite enjoyed helping heroes complete their varied quests), removed its teeth and planted them as though they were seeds. From those tooth-seeds sprang fully grown men called the Spartoi (in Greek mythology, people who sprang from the earth itself were called *autochthones*—they were original to the earth rather than being settlers or colonizers). The Spartoi men immediately fought one another, and eventually only five remained. These five remaining men, along with Cadmus, became the first citizens of the new city of Thebes, and from them all Thebans were believed to be descended.

Next, Cadmus married the goddess Harmonia (a rare instance of a mortal marrying a goddess!). Harmonia was the daughter of Aphrodite and Ares and so was a child of the goddess of beauty and love and the god of war. She was beautiful and strong, and together with Cadmus she ruled over the city of Thebes for a generation. At the wedding, all the gods were in attendance (which, again, was *very* rare; see Paris's entry for the only other instance of this). Harmonia was gifted with a necklace from her stepfather, Hephaestus. Probably due to Hephaestus's anger and jealousy at yet another child from the incessant unions of his wife, Aphrodite, and Ares, the necklace was cursed. The curse didn't affect Cadmus and Harmonia themselves, but it went on to cause great tragedy for their children and grandchildren.

Eventually Cadmus and Harmonia left Thebes and wandered together until they reached Illyria. There, they were transformed by the gods into snakes. This wasn't punishment, though it sounds like one—instead, it was meant to allow them to live out the rest of their lives safely away from the tragedy that would continue to befall their family.

Now You Know

The mythology of Cadmus tells that it was he who brought the alphabet from Phoenicia to the Greek world. Most of Greek mythology credits Cadmus as being the father of the ancient Greek alphabet. The Phoenicians, historically, went on to found cities throughout northern Africa, including what became the city of Carthage. The Carthaginians were one of ancient Rome's biggest rivals and feature in Rome's founding story, the *Aeneid*.

ATALANTA

A Heroine of Arcadia (or, Some Say, Boeotia)

What's Her Deal?

Atalanta is the only *official* heroine (to the extent any hero was official!) of ancient Greece—meaning, the only woman designated a hero by the same standards that classify Perseus, Heracles, and the others. There are, of course, other strong, independent, and brave women of Greek mythology, but she is the only one who got to be called a heroine.

Atalanta was born either in Arcadia or Boeotia, and either to one set of parents or another, depending on the variation. According to some stories, there were two women named Atalanta who did almost exactly the same things with their lives, but more likely there were two versions of her, possibly because two regions wanted to claim Atalanta as their own.

Regardless of where Atalanta was born or who her parents were, the story goes that her father was incredibly disappointed when she was born a girl and not a boy. He was so disappointed that he left her outside to die, exposed to the elements. Instead of dying, however, she was found and nursed by a bear. This early life led her to be brave, strong, and skilled with weapons, namely a bow and arrow.

The practice of death by exposure was common in Greek mythology (it also happened to Oedipus and Paris). Unwanted children (or those with a prophecy against their favor) were left, usually on a mountainside, to be killed by the elements or wild animals. They never died in the stories, though—instead, the process acted as a means of strengthening them or hiding their familial origins for use in later drama.

The Story You Need to Know

Atalanta is best known for her role in the famed Calydonian Boar Hunt. The Calydonian Boar was a monstrous creature sent by Artemis to punish the king of Calydon, who'd neglected to properly worship the goddess. The boar tore apart the region, killing cattle and even the men who tried to stop it. Finally, the king had to do something about it. He put out the call for the strongest and bravest of Greece to come help him get rid of the Calydonian Boar.

A group of heroes arrived to help the king. They sailed on the ship called the *Argo* and so went by the name the Argonauts (see Jason's entry for more). Along with the other Argonauts (including Castor and Polydeuces, Peleus, and even Theseus!), Atalanta arrived in Calydon ready to help the king with his boar problem. She made quite the entrance as a woman arriving in full armor among a host of men. Immediately, Atalanta caught the eye of the king's son, Meleager. Meleager was completely taken with Atalanta, but she wasn't interested. While Meleager supported her joining the hunt and always tried to impress Atalanta, many of the other men weren't thrilled to be hunting with a woman (women in ancient Greece weren't expected to do much outside the home). Meleager, though, insisted that the men include Atalanta as if she were one of them.

The group went in search of the boar and soon found it. It killed two of the men in an instant. The group was in a panic—well, all but Atalanta, who was calm and collected as she aimed her arrow at the boar. Atalanta hit the boar, the first of the group to wound it. The beast was stunned by her shot, and Meleager rushed in and stabbed it. While Meleager *technically* killed the animal, even he recognized he couldn't have done it without Atalanta's arrow. He convinced the other men of the hunt to award the boar's skin to Atalanta as a trophy in recognition of her skill in the hunt. Meleager's own brothers were so angry about this that they tried to prevent him from awarding it to her. Meleager killed them and returned the boar's skin to Atalanta.

Now You Know

When Meleager was first born, the Fates told his mother that as soon as a particular piece of wood (that she'd just thrown onto the fire!) was fully burned, her son would die. His mother took the wood off the fire immediately, doused it in water, and hid it away for safety. But when Meleager killed his brothers in the name of a woman, his mother was so furious with him that she retrieved the wood from where she'd hidden it and tossed it on the fire. When it had finally burned up, Meleager fell to the ground, dead.

DAEDALUS

An Inventor from Athens

ᒫᒪᒫᒪᒫᒪᒫᒪ

What's His Deal?

Daedalus was an inventor originally from Athens who descended from the city's early kings. He was Greek mythology's most famous inventor, revered for his skills and his ability to create almost anything (both brilliant, ingenious inventions and super weird ones).

Daedalus appears in Disney's *Hercules* (the TV series) as the father of Hercules's best friend, Icarus (Icarus refers to Daedalus as "Dad-alus"). The father and son are also frequently depicted in artwork, songs, and literature, usually surrounding the tragic fall of Icarus.

The Story You Need to Know

Daedalus was renowned and sought after for his abilities to invent things. He was so good at what he did that his sister, Perdix, asked him if he would teach her son, Daedalus's nephew, Talos, how to be an inventor as well. Daedalus was happy to—he wanted to spread his knowledge and was flattered to be asked. Daedalus was a good inventor, but he also *knew* he was a good inventor: He had an ego.

Talos was a quick learner and proved to be incredibly talented in his own right. He took to inventing right away and without any help from Daedalus came up with the saw (he was inspired by the spine of a fish, taking a strip of metal and adding serrated teeth) and the compass (the kind used for math; he fastened two pointed pieces of metal together to measure and draw circles). These were brilliant inventions that would be widely used. Because of his nephew's success, Daedalus found himself feeling overshadowed and jealous. One day when he was teaching Talos, Daedalus's jealousy and frustration with the boy's inherent skills bubbled over, and he pushed him off the cliffs of the Acropolis.

Daedalus was caught and exiled for his crimes. He traveled through Greece before finally ending up on the island of Crete, where he became the resident inventor for King Minos and Queen Pasiphaë. Eventually, Daedalus created a contraption that allowed Pasiphaë to become impregnated by Poseidon's bull, resulting in the Minotaur (see the entry on Pasiphaë and Minos for more on that very icky invention), and as a result Minos punished Daedalus. He had him create the Labyrinth to contain the Minotaur and then forced Daedalus to remain inside the Labyrinth, trapping him in his own invention for his role in what Minos saw as Pasiphaë's betrayal. The Labyrinth of Knossos, on Crete, was said to be completely inescapable. It wasn't like the labyrinths or mazes we think of today—this one had thousands of possible routes. It was used to house the Minotaur because it kept the beast safely contained and unable to harm the people of Knossos. To help feed the creature, Minos would force fourteen Athenian youths to enter every seven years, and the Minotaur would slowly feed off of them as they came upon him. While Daedalus was living on the island of Crete, he developed a relationship with one of Minos's enslaved servants, a woman named Naucrate. Together they had a son, Icarus.

Now You Know

When Daedalus pushed Talos off the cliff in Athens, Athena was watching. As the boy fell, she decided to save him in whatever way she could. She transformed Talos into a partridge before he hit the ground. The ancient Greeks believed this was why the partridge remained low to the ground and wasn't able to fly like most birds—Talos was left afraid of heights.

Icarus

The Son of Daedalus

———◆———

Icarus was imprisoned with his father when Minos punished Daedalus for his role in Pasiphaë's relationship with the bull of Poseidon. It isn't clear what happened to Icarus's mother, Naucrate, during this time, though she wasn't with Icarus and Daedalus when they were trapped inside Daedalus's own invention, the Labyrinth. Even Daedalus couldn't get himself out of his own creation, and it was only with the help of Pasiphaë that the two were able to escape. Pasiphaë felt bad for Daedalus's punishment, given he had been following her instructions, so she freed the two and allowed them to hide out while they planned their escape from the island of Crete.

Daedalus set out trying to determine the best way for them to get off the island and make it to the mainland. They couldn't take a ship—Minos had an incredible fleet of boats, but it was very well protected and they would never be able to steal a ship without anyone noticing. The only other option, Daedalus determined, was flight. They would have to find a way to fly off the island.

Daedalus began to build a set of wings for him and his son. First, he made a wooden skeleton, imitating that of the larger birds he was able to examine on the island. On the skeleton, he attached feathers. He found exactly the right size of feathers by scouring the land—the wings had to be precisely like those of a bird or else they wouldn't work. It was planned intricately: Daedalus was able to sew the larger feathers onto the skeleton so they were securely fastened, but he applied the smaller feathers with wax, as they were too small to be sewn.

Finally, the wings were complete. Daedalus showed Icarus how to use the wings, exactly how to flap and how often; he explained that Icarus could not, for any reason, fly so low over the water that the wings got wet, because that would ruin them and he would fall to his death. He also explained that Icarus was not to fly too high, because if he got too close to the sun the wax holding on the smaller feathers would melt and, again, he would fall

to his death. With the rules and regulations figured out, Daedalus attached his son's wings, and then his own, and they took flight.

They flew smoothly for a while—the wings were working just as planned. But the longer they flew, the more restless Icarus became. After all, he was young, and the constant flapping and flying straight was getting boring. Icarus decided he could have a little bit of fun, so he varied his flight pattern to make the journey far more exciting. Daedalus chastised his son for taking the risk. But Icarus was stubborn, and he continued to have fun with his flying, going lower and then higher. He felt invincible, like he knew what he was doing. But before long, he flew too high and too close to the sun. The wax on Icarus's wings began to melt, just as Daedalus had warned him, and he fell. Crying out for his father, Icarus fell into the sea and died. Daedalus mourned for his son and buried his body on the closest island before he had to continue on, successfully flying all the way to Sicily.

The region of the Mediterranean where Icarus is said to have fallen is named for him. It is the Icarian Sea, and the nearest island to where Icarus is said to have fallen is called Icaria.

PASIPHAË and MINOS

A Queen and King of Knossos, Crete

᠎᠎᠎᠎᠎᠎

What's Their Deal?

Pasiphaë and Minos were queen and king of Knossos on the island of Crete. Pasiphaë was the daughter of Helios, the Titan and god of the sun, and the nymph Perseis. Minos was the son of Zeus and Europa. Their reign on Crete was marked by the existence of the Minotaur, half man and half bull. The beast lived within the famous Labyrinth, built by Daedalus, and periodically feasted on unlucky groups of Athenian youth.

Pasiphaë was the sister of the witch goddess Circe and features in the novel *Circe* by Madeline Miller, in a visceral retelling of the birth of the Minotaur. Minos, after his death, became a judge in the Underworld.

The Story You Need to Know

When Minos took over as king of Knossos (a position he fought his brothers for), he was eager to prove to the Cretan people that he deserved to be their king. He announced that it was determined by the gods themselves that he would, and should, be king (his father was, after all, Zeus). As proof of this, Minos prayed to the god Poseidon to send a bull to the people of Crete as a sign of his rightful place as their king. He assured the god in his prayers that he would sacrifice the bull when it appeared to him.

Poseidon did indeed send a bull. Almost immediately, a beautiful bull arose from the sea, ready to be sacrificed just as Minos had promised to the god. But the bull was...impressive and so stunning that Minos just couldn't bring himself to sacrifice it! Instead, he sacrificed another bull that he had on hand (there are *a lot* of bulls in Crete's myths) and let Poseidon's bull live. This act of defiance was incredibly offensive to the god, and as punishment, he caused Minos's wife, Pasiphaë, to fall in love with the bull that Minos had neglected to sacrifice. This was not love in the way a human loves their pet; Pasiphaë developed a passionate, sexual love for the bull of Poseidon. She immediately found herself wanting to have sex with the bull and sought to find a way to make that possible.

On the island of Crete lived the inventor Daedalus (see his and Icarus's entries for more). He was incredibly talented and able to create almost anything if he set his mind to it. Pasiphaë enlisted Daedalus to create something with which she could fulfill her desires for the bull. Daedalus, eager to continue to prove his superiority in inventing, took on the task, disturbing as it may have been. Daedalus created a large wooden cow. He covered it in real cowhide, and it looked very much like a real cow, except it was hollow. It had just enough space inside for a woman to hide.

Just as intended, Pasiphaë used the hollow wooden cow created by Daedalus to have sex with the bull of Poseidon and eventually became pregnant with the Minotaur, half bull, half man. This act was seen by Minos as a betrayal, and he punished Daedalus for his role in it. In truth, though, it was Minos's neglect of Poseidon that caused the whole mess in the first place.

Now You Know

After these events, the bull of Poseidon began ravaging the island of Crete, where it became known as the Cretan Bull. It was eventually stopped by Heracles, who brought it to the Greek mainland. There, it began ravaging the region of Marathon, then becoming known as the Marathonian Bull, before it was finally sacrificed in a show of power by the hero Theseus.

The Minotaur

A Monstrous Half Man, Half Bull

AKA: Asterius; Asterion

———◆———

The Minotaur was the child of Pasiphaë's forced love with Poseidon's bull and punishment for Minos choosing not to sacrifice the bull as he had promised to the god. The Minotaur's given name was Asterius (or Asterion), which means "the starry one." When

the Minotaur was born, those around him immediately realized that he must be contained. While many half-human creatures of mythology retained human characteristics, the Minotaur was monstrous and vicious. Unlike many half-human species, the Minotaur's top half was a bull (or sometimes just the head, and in those cases he had very distinctly human abs!), and he therefore didn't seem to have retained any kind of human cognition: no thoughts, feelings, or empathy. He was, simply, a monster.

> While the Minotaur is completely mythological, the people of Bronze Age Crete (one of the earliest Greek civilizations) used bull iconography heavily. There were bulls painted *everywhere*, including paintings of Cretan youth leaping over bulls.

Minos and Pasiphaë were so afraid of the Minotaur's ferocity that they had Daedalus create a means of containing him. Daedalus built the Labyrinth, in which the Minotaur could stay far away from the Cretan people but could still be regularly fed. The Labyrinth was a massive maze that even Daedalus, its creator, couldn't find his way out of. It also served to hide the Minotaur away, thus hiding the shame of Minos.

Around this time, Minos waged war against Athens and was about to beat the city horribly. Instead the two sides came to an agreement: Minos would relent, and the Athenians would send seven young men and seven young women to Crete every seven years. These young people would become the victims of the Minotaur.

It was only when the hero Theseus, a prince of Athens, volunteered to be one of these Athenian youths that the Minotaur was finally defeated. Theseus traveled to Crete as one of its victims, then seduced a princess of Crete, Ariadne, and convinced her to help him. Ariadne gave Theseus thread that he could use to track his path through the Labyrinth and to the Minotaur. Once he had killed the monster, he was able to follow the thread back the way he had come and escape the Labyrinth, something that had not been possible for anyone else who had entered it.

ORPHEUS AND EURYDICE

A Young Musician and a Beautiful Young Woman

52525252

What's Their Deal?

Orpheus was a young man from Thrace and the son of a Thracian king and the Muse Calliope. Orpheus took after his mother and was considered the best mortal poet and musician ever to live (he was second only to the gods themselves!). When he played the lyre, everyone within hearing distance was taken with his music and, by extension, with him. He could command attention from anyone by playing a single note. Orpheus took part in the quest for the Golden Fleece, accompanying Jason and the Argonauts and using his musical skills wherever he could.

When Orpheus was on the *Argo*, he saved the other sailors from the Sirens' dangerous calls. When they sang their enchanting song, Orpheus played his own lyre so loudly and beautifully that it drowned out the Siren song that would have otherwise doomed the ship and everyone on board.

Orpheus married the young woman Eurydice. Sadly, we don't know much about her other than that he loved her very much, and, one can assume based on their story, she loved him too.

The Story You Need to Know

When Orpheus returned from his voyage on the *Argo* with Jason and the other Argonauts, he settled down in his homeland in Thrace and married the beautiful young woman Eurydice. The couple had been married for only a day or two when Eurydice was wandering in a meadow with some of her friends and was bitten by a poisonous snake. Tragically, the young bride died right there.

Orpheus was drowned by his grief, overwhelmed by his love for this woman who had died so very early in their life together. He was determined to do anything he could to bring her back to him (whether such a strong drive was a strength or a flaw is open to interpretation). Orpheus decided that he would travel all the way to the Underworld and convince the king and queen of the dead to relinquish their hold on Eurydice. This was not an easy quest—there was a reason it wasn't attempted more often. Even if a person could get to the Underworld, Hades and Persephone were not easily convinced.

When Orpheus did reach the Underworld (we don't know much about his journey to get there) he began to play his lyre. He played such beautiful and calming music that he brought the whole of the Underworld to a standstill. Charon, the ferryman who shepherded the dead to their new home, was charmed into allowing Orpheus across the river. Cerberus, the vicious three-headed dog that guarded the entrance to the world of the dead, was lulled to sleep. The place was so calmed by Orpheus's incredible tune that even the perpetual tortures ceased for a time. For example, the tortures of men like Ixion, Tantalus, and even Sisyphus, who pushed a boulder up a hill only for it to roll back down for eternity, had a brief respite.

Just like the rest of the Underworld around them, King Hades and Queen Persephone were moved by Orpheus's music and granted his request to bring his wife back to the world of the living. There was one condition: Orpheus was not to look back at Eurydice until they had left the Underworld completely—he could not lay eyes upon his wife until they were fully in the land of the living. Orpheus eagerly agreed, and Eurydice was brought to follow him as they made their way back from the Underworld.

Orpheus wanted desperately to glance briefly behind him, just to be sure that no trick had been played on him and that he really would soon have Eurydice back! He refrained, though, pushing back his urges until he finally reached the daylight of the world above. He'd successfully made his way out of the Underworld! The moment he was standing in that precious daylight, he turned, excited to see his wife in the flesh. But it was too soon—Orpheus was free from the Underworld, but Eurydice still had a couple of steps before she was in the daylight too. He saw his wife for a brief second before she was pulled back to the world of the dead, able only to utter the word *goodbye* before she disappeared completely.

Now You Know

The character of Orpheus changed drastically over the generations of the ancient world. There eventually developed an Orphic Tradition, religious rites based around Orpheus that reimagined the origin of the gods and the mythology as a whole.

PHAETHON

Son of the Titan Helios and the Nymph Clymene

5252525252

What's His Deal?

Phaethon was the son of the Titan Helios and the nymph Clymene. Helios was god of the sun, thus he controlled it: Every day he drove a chariot that pulled the sun across the sky (Helios was also, in some traditions, the sun itself). Phaethon had seven sisters known as Heliades (daughters of Helios).

The first episode of Disney's *Hercules* (the TV series) features Hercules in the same role as Phaethon. He's allowed to drive the sun chariot (though the show uses the later mythology of Apollo as the sun god) and does about as much damage as Phaethon.

The Story You Need to Know

Phaethon, whose name means "shining," was a child of the shining sun god Helios. Phaethon was young and boastful, bragging to his friends about the importance of his father, who brought the sun across the sky. But Phaethon's friends found it hard to believe his claims and told him so. Their doubt was hard to take. …Being a teenager is hard enough without your friends refusing to believe your father drives the sun chariot! Phaethon felt it was necessary to prove it to his friends—he wanted to make perfectly clear that it really was his father who drove the sun across the sky.

In order to prove it, Phaethon needed to speak to his father. Helios was, for the most part, an absent father (he was a little busy), so when Phaethon arrived to speak with him, Helios promised him whatever he wanted, all before Phaethon was even able to speak a word. This was perfect! Phaethon proceeded to ask him if, maybe, some time, he might be able to drive the chariot across the sky? Just this once? Helios was hesitant, because this was an incredibly dangerous request. It was *the sun*, after all—it wasn't easy to move, and Phaethon was so young and inexperienced. But Helios had already promised him! He was bound to follow through, as much as he now regretted that decision. He told Phaethon this, in the hopes that his son would take back the request. But Phaethon didn't relent. Phaethon felt that if he could only drive the sun chariot, he would be able to prove to his friends who his father was, and everything in his life would be easier! So, Helios agreed.

Before Phaethon was allowed to go out in the chariot, Helios warned him of *everything* he could think of: Where to go, how to get there, what to avoid (don't go too low! or too high!); he warned him how tricky it could be to control the horses, and so on. Finally, Helios had done all that he could to prepare his son for the journey across the sky, though he was still horribly anxious at the thought. Helios smeared some magical salve across Phaethon's face to protect him from the sun's rays, and with that he let Phaethon take off in the chariot with the sun pulled closely behind.

It seemed to go well at first, but it wasn't long before Phaethon panicked and everything went wrong at once. Phaethon lost control of the chariot completely, and it flew off course, going this way and that, pulling the sun along with it and setting half the earth on fire. The earth burned and burned as the chariot roared out of control, covering the lands in flames. Finally, it was so bad and so unstoppable that Zeus had to put an end to the havoc being wreaked by the sun chariot. He threw a lightning bolt at Phaethon, stopping the chariot in its tracks.

Phaethon fell to the earth; the poor boy was dead. Where he landed, his sisters, the Heliades, mourned for him, crying for their brother until they were transformed into poplar trees.

Now You Know

Part of the Phaethon story involved him flying too close to the earth as he flew over southeast Asia and Africa. This, the myth claims, is why the people of those regions had darker skin than those of Greece.

OEDIPUS

A Prince of Both Thebes and Corinth

⌐⌐⌐⌐⌐⌐

What's His Deal?

Oedipus was a prince of Thebes, born to King Laius and Queen Jocasta. As a prince of Thebes, Oedipus was one of the many cursed descendants of Cadmus and Harmonia. He later became a prince of Corinth and then the king of Thebes (it's a long story). Oedipus is most famous for the "complex" named for him, and for the actions around his story, though it's rare that people properly recall the story in its entirety. The story itself is most frequently retold through *Oedipus Tyrannos* (*Oedipus Rex* in Latin): *Oedipus the King*, the ancient play by Sophocles. Oedipus and his family also appear in the more recent adaptation *The Children of Jocasta*, a novel by Natalie Haynes.

The Story You Need to Know

Oedipus was born to the king and queen of Thebes. Laius, his father, learned of a prophecy that Oedipus would grow up to kill him, and so he made the decision to expose the baby (leave him on a mountainside and let the animals or elements kill him). But the servant sent to expose the baby couldn't go through with it. Instead, he gave the baby to a shepherd, who brought him to the city of Corinth, where he was adopted by the king and queen. In Corinth, Oedipus grew up as any other prince, except for a rumor that he wasn't the blood child of his Corinthian parents. When he was old enough, Oedipus traveled to the Oracle and he, too, learned of a prophecy. This one said that one day he would kill his father and marry his mother (quite the fate to learn!). Oedipus was so disturbed by this prophecy that he vowed never to return to Corinth (he ignored the earlier rumor about his parents, which could've solved all his problems before they started!).

Instead, Oedipus went to the crossroads between Corinth and Thebes to figure out where to go next. At those crossroads, he got into a road rage altercation with a man in a chariot. Oedipus's anger got the best of him, and he ended up killing the man at the crossroads. He continued on the road, finally coming to the Sphinx (a lion with the upper half of a woman and an eagle's wings). The Sphinx had a riddle for Oedipus, and unless he solved it, he couldn't pass by (the Sphinx had a habit of killing those who couldn't answer correctly). Though he had trouble controlling his temper, Oedipus was a smart guy, and he answered the Sphinx's riddle and was able to pass into the city. It turned out the city of Thebes had been plagued by the Sphinx for so long that the Thebans were absolutely thrilled to see Oedipus! Their king had just been killed, and between that and the Sphinx killing everyone who passed it on the road, they were in desperate need of some good news. Oedipus was welcomed into the city by the recently widowed queen, Jocasta, and the pair got along famously.

Here is the Sphinx's riddle: What walks on four feet in the morning, two in the afternoon, and three in the evening? The answer: humans! (Babies crawl on all fours, adults walk on two legs, and the elderly use a cane.)

Oedipus and Jocasta quickly became closer and closer, eventually falling in love and getting married. Together they had four children: Antigone, Ismene, Eteocles, and Polynices. Oedipus and Jocasta were a happy couple for a long time, raising their children in Thebes—things were going well. But when their children were in their teens, this all changed when a plague ravaged Thebes. People began dying at horrible rates, and Oedipus set out to figure out why it was happening. Plagues were controlled by Apollo, so Oedipus sent his brother-in-law, Creon, to the Oracle to seek guidance. There Creon learned that the plague was affecting Thebes because the murderer of Laius hadn't been punished for his crimes.

At first, Oedipus couldn't imagine who the murderer could be. But when more details about the death of Laius were revealed, Oedipus learned it was he himself who had killed Laius at the crossroads. And not only that; he eventually learned that he was the child of Laius and Jocasta. So, not only had he killed the king of Thebes without knowing; he had fulfilled the prophecy he was so afraid of: He'd killed his father and married his mother. In her grief and horror, Jocasta took her own life. In his own shame, Oedipus gouged out his eyes before exiling himself from Thebes. His daughter Antigone then acted as his eyes, guiding him through his wanderings until his death.

Now You Know

A common idea surrounding Oedipus is that he *knew*, even just subconsciously, that he was killing his father and marrying his mother. This is where Freud's complex comes from, but neither of these ideas make sense. Oedipus couldn't have known the man on the crossroads was his father, nor could he have known the widowed queen was his mother. When he learned, he was horrified.

PROCNE AND PHILOMELA

Two Sisters of the Royal House of Athens

ᒲᒷᒲᒷᒲᒷᒲᒷ

What's Their Deal?

Procne and Philomela were two daughters of one of the earliest kings of Athens, Erechtheus. They were known for being part of an ancient generation of Athenian royalty but were most famous for the abject tragedy they endured in their lifetimes. The two sisters were saved from further tragedy when the gods turned them into a nightingale and a swallow, respectively.

The Story You Need to Know

Procne, the older of the two sisters, was married to a man named Tereus. Together they lived in his homeland of Thrace. Tereus was a son of Ares, the god of war. Procne had been given to Tereus in marriage and missed her home of Athens and her family horribly. Procne missed her beloved sister, Philomela, most of all.

Procne and Tereus had a son named Itys, and Procne wanted so badly to introduce her sister to the child while he was still young. She begged her husband to let her invite Philomela to Thrace to visit, and he agreed. Tereus decided to go to Athens himself to collect Philomela. Tereus, though, was an absolutely *awful* man, and as soon as he met Philomela, he just *had* to have her (in addition to her sister).

On their way back to Thrace, the pair stopped to rest. There, Tereus told Philomela that he'd received the news that her sister had died (this was, of course, a complete lie). Philomela was horrified and ruined by grief. While she wallowed in sorrow, Tereus forced her into a sham marriage in an attempt to solidify his desire to be married to both sisters. Before long, though, Philomela realized the truth: Her sister was alive, and this horrible man had forced her into an illegitimate marriage. Philomela, furious, threatened Tereus. He responded to her threat by cutting out her tongue and hiding her away where she couldn't escape. He then continued on home and told his wife, Procne, that her sister had died.

Philomela was determined to free herself from Tereus's imprisonment and reach her sister. She couldn't speak because of what he'd done to her, but she could still weave and was given a loom (a major oversight on Tereus's part). Philomela wove an intricate scene that depicted exactly what had happened to her—everything Tereus had done to her and how he had silenced her. Once the tapestry was finished, she gave it to a woman who checked in on her and told her to bring it to Procne.

When Procne looked at the tapestry, she immediately understood what was being conveyed to her. Philomela had incredible talent, and Procne now knew the horror her own husband had inflicted on her beloved sister. Procne began to plot how she would punish her husband for what he'd done.

First, Procne freed her sister. Shortly after, she came upon her son, Itys, and realized what she had to do. She killed her son, cut him into small pieces, and served the child to her husband for his dinner. After Tereus had eaten what he didn't know was his own son, she told him. Tereus was stunned long enough for the women to get a head start fleeing from him. Eventually, Tereus caught up with them, though, and was about to kill the sisters when the gods intervened. Procne was transformed into a nightingale, and Philomela into a swallow.

The ancient Greeks believed that the swallow could only twitter, never sing like other birds, so it was appropriate that Philomela, who had been silenced by Tereus, became this bird.

Now You Know

The punishment Procne inflicted on Tereus for his crimes is similar to that of Medea's punishment for Jason. Women had very little power in ancient Greece, and the power they did have revolved around their ability to produce children and heirs for men. Thus, while it may seem unimaginable, the most powerful thing they could do to punish men for horrific crimes was to commit one themselves: They could take away the man's heir and, in doing so, his ability to carry on his name.

TANTALUS
AND HIS FAMILY

A King of Lydia and His Cursed Family

AKA: The Tantalids

᠎᠎᠎

What's Their Deal?

Tantalus was a king of Lydia whose transgressions against the gods brought a curse on his family that would last generations. The family is sometimes referred to as the Tantalids (children of Tantalus). The word *tantalize* comes from the story of Tantalus and the punishment inflicted upon him. He is forever tantalized in the Underworld, never able to fulfill his desires.

The curse on Tantalus's family is sometimes called the Tantalid Curse, the Curse on the Pelopidai, or the Curse on the House of Atreus (so many name options prove *just how cursed* this family was!).

The Story You Need to Know

The curse began with Tantalus, a son of Zeus. He was respected by the gods—so respected that they invited him to sit at their dinner table (a very rare occurrence when it comes to mortals). This first dinner went well, and so the gods decided they would join Tantalus at his own table for another momentous dinner. On that occasion, Tantalus chose to test the gods. He killed his son Pelops, cut him up, and boiled the pieces into a stew that he proceeded to feed to the gods. The gods realized there was something wrong with their meal, but not before Demeter had taken a single bite. They punished Tantalus for his crime, sending him to the depths of the Underworld, Tartarus, where he would forever be tantalized by food and water that were just out of reach. Pelops, meanwhile, was restored to his body (he was given an ivory shoulder to replace the bite Demeter had taken!).

Pelops grew up unaffected by the curse on his father's house. He eventually sought a wife, Hippodamia, whom he had to win via a chariot race with her father. The race was rigged in his favor, some say by Hippodamia herself. That story claims that Hippodamia had her father's charioteer, Myrtilus, pull the pin from his chariot's wheels, thus allowing Pelops to win with ease. Later, Pelops killed Myrtilus, throwing him off a cliff. Myrtilus cursed Pelops as he fell (adding yet another curse on the Tantalid family!).

The next stage of the curse lies with Tantalus's daughter, Niobe, whose story is told in the entry on Leto. After that, the curse transferred to Pelops's two sons, Atreus and Thyestes, who fought over the throne of Mycenae. Thyestes made a move on Atreus's wife, which caused Atreus to punish him by (in the same vein as his grandfather) killing Thyestes's children, boiling them, and serving them to Thyestes as a meal. Punishment came for this crime, but it wasn't served on Atreus. Instead, his children lived out the curse on the family. Menelaus and Agamemnon were the sons of Atreus, and Aegisthus was the son of Thyestes (born after the death of the other children). Menelaus's wife, Helen, was kidnapped by a prince of Troy, thus sparking the famous Trojan War. Agamemnon, however, suffered the brunt of the curse. In order to gain favorable wind for the journey to Troy, Agamemnon had sacrificed his own daughter Iphigenia. For this, his wife, along with his cousin, Aegisthus, spent the ten-year-long war plotting revenge (Aegisthus's desire for revenge had more to do with the actions of Agamemnon's father). When Agamemnon returned home, they killed him, a story told in more detail in the entry on Clytemnestra and Her Children.

Now You Know

One of the worst things a person could do in ancient Greek mythology was any form of cannibalism. It was sometimes used as a punishment, other times as a kind of sick test (as in the case of Tantalus). Another example is included in the entry on Procne and Philomela. When it involved the gods, it was even more horrific and always resulted in the most incredible of curses.

THE DANAIDS

Fifty Daughters of Danaüs

52525252

What's Their Deal?

The Danaids were fifty women, daughters of a man named Danaüs. They were originally from Africa and said to be descendants of Io, whose wanderings took her to the Nile. The women are famous for the punishment inflicted upon them. They spent eternity in the Underworld, where they perpetually filled their basins with water only to have it drain out before it could be transported anywhere.

The Story You Need to Know

The story of the fifty Danaids begins in Africa and the Middle East, where a king, Belus, assigned his two sons to new kingdoms. His son Aegyptus would be the king of Egypt and the land to the east, into modern Lebanon (according to some, he named it Egypt after himself). Danaüs would be the king of what the ancient Greeks called Libya (this was most of North Africa, west of Egypt). When Belus died, though, the brothers fought over what their father had left them.

As a truce, Aegyptus proposed that his fifty sons marry their fifty cousins, the Danaids, Danaüs's fifty daughters. The Danaids, though, were absolutely opposed to the marriage and would do anything to prevent it from happening. Whether they suspected some kind of trap among the brothers or simply didn't want to marry the men, the Danaids fled Egypt and traveled across the sea, where they landed in the city of Argos, in Greece.

At this time, Argos was experiencing a horrible drought, said to be caused by Poseidon in his anger at Hera for becoming the patron goddess of the city. The Danaids went in search of water when one of them, Amymone, threw a spear and accidentally hit a sleeping satyr. The satyr, angry and surprised, prepared to assault Amymone when Poseidon appeared and stopped the satyr before assaulting Amymone himself. When he was finished, Poseidon showed Amymone to the springs of Lerna as a sick sort of "thank you." The city of Argos was saved from its drought.

Shortly after the drought ended, the fifty sons of Aegyptus found the Danaids and Danaüs in Argos and, once again, proposed to marry them. Neither the daughters nor Danaüs had changed their minds about the proposed marriage, but this time, the Danaids had no way of getting out of the marriage, and the festivities were prepared. It's not clear why or how they were forced into it, but they were. On the day of the wedding, Danaüs gave each of his daughters a small dagger that she could hide in her clothes during the ceremony. The Danaids tucked their new, very sharp daggers neatly away within their dresses. The ceremony was performed, and the Danaids were married off to the fifty sons of their uncle, Aegyptus.

On the night of their weddings, each of the fifty Danaids went off with each of their new husbands to their bedrooms. When the husbands had fallen asleep, one by one, each of the Danaids stabbed each of their husbands to death. All except one: Hypermnestra couldn't bring herself to kill the young man Lynceus, who lay peacefully sleeping next to her. She woke him, and he fled Argos. Hypermnestra was imprisoned by Danaüs for letting Lynceus live.

Meanwhile, the rest of the Danaids buried the heads of their husbands by the spring at Lerna and held funerals for their bodies in Argos. Upon their deaths, the Danaids were given eternal punishments in the Underworld. They had to endlessly carry water, only for it to drain out of the basins they held.

Now You Know

Along with Tantalus, Ixion (see Hera's entry), and the famous Sisyphus, punished with perpetually pushing a boulder up a hill only to have it roll back down, the Danaids were some of the most famous residents of Tartarus in the Underworld, where they lived out their eternal punishments.

PARIS

A Prince of Troy

AKA: Alexander; Alexandros (alternate spelling)

ᒲᒲᒲᒲᒲᒲ

What's His Deal?

Paris was a prince of Troy, the son of King Priam and Queen Hecuba, and the brother of the famous hero of the Trojan War, Hector. When he was born, Paris was removed from the royal household and exposed, left to die in the mountains. Hecuba had dreamed that he would cause the city of Troy to burn, so she exposed him in an attempt to avoid that fate. Paris didn't die, though—he survived and was raised by a shepherd before eventually returning to his family in Troy as though the prophecy had been forgotten entirely (guess how that turns out?).

You might know Paris from the 2004 movie *Troy*, in which his romance with Helen is portrayed as very real and very passionate. It's an incredibly romanticized interpretation of their story, the truth of which is unclear.

The Story You Need to Know

When Paris was a young man, he was brought in by the gods to settle an argument that was called the Judgment of Paris.

Years earlier, there had been a wedding: The hero Peleus was marrying the goddess Thetis, and all the gods and other deities were invited...except Eris, the goddess of strife and discord (she was *not fun*). Proving the point entirely, Eris crashed the party anyway. She arrived at the wedding uninvited and bearing a gift: a golden apple. It wasn't meant for the bride or groom, though. Instead, she tossed the apple toward three goddesses who were gathered together: Hera, Athena, and Aphrodite. On the apple was inscribed the phrase "for the fairest." Each of the three goddesses firmly believed that she was the fairest and therefore the apple was meant for her! An argument ensued—Hera, Athena, and Aphrodite could be very stubborn, especially when it came to proving one of them was better than the others.

Eris is rarely mentioned in the mythology, but when she is, she is quite the force! She essentially started the Trojan War, and during the fighting she rode through the battlefield screaming for bloodshed.

Eventually the argument over the golden apple (known as the Apple of Discord) got so heated that Zeus was brought in to settle it. Zeus looked at his wife, his favorite daughter, and the goddess of love and realized there was no way he was going to make that call. It was just not worth it! Instead, he set the decision to be made in the future by a young man of Troy named Paris.

When the time came, Hermes found Paris, and the Trojan was brought before Zeus, Hera, Athena, and Aphrodite and asked to finally, after all that time, settle the argument of *who is the fairest?* Each goddess pleaded her case: Hera offered Paris power—she said she would make him a powerful king if he chose her as the fairest. Athena offered him success in war—she told him that he'd never lose a battle if he chose her. Aphrodite offered him love or, rather, a woman—she offered Paris the most beautiful woman in the world.

Paris chose Aphrodite; he was a young man and nothing sounded better than a gorgeous woman! With the decision made, it was revealed that the most beautiful woman in the world was a woman named Helen, who just happened to be currently married to the king of Sparta, Menelaus.

With Helen promised to Paris by the goddess of love herself, Paris felt he had every right to take her by force. Paris stole Helen away in the night, and they were long gone by the time Menelaus realized they were missing. It's not known whether or not Helen went willingly—women in ancient Greece didn't have a lot of say in anything, but she *could* have chosen to go with him. Either way, Paris and Helen "honeymooned" on a Greek island for a while before returning to Troy to face the music. Meanwhile, Menelaus went to his brother, Agamemnon, to decide what to do as retribution for this slight. Agamemnon voted for war (see his and Achilles and Patroclus's entries for the Trojan War).

Now You Know

Paris is portrayed as pretty spoiled and entitled, and choosing Aphrodite in the Judgment of Paris certainly helped reinforce that description. Even when the Trojan War was going on and Trojans were dying by the handful, Paris tried to stay as far away from the fray as possible and left the fighting up to his brother, Hector, the real hero of Troy during the war.

AGAMEMNON

King of Mycenae; Leader of the Greeks During the Trojan War

᠎᠎᠎᠎᠎᠎

What's His Deal?

Agamemnon was the king of Mycenae; brother to Menelaus, the king of Sparta (who got the kingship by marrying Helen, the princess of Sparta); and a member of the House of Atreus, a family cursed with absolutely horrible fates (see the entry on Tantalus and His Family, where *a lot* went down).

Agamemnon was the leader of the Greek army that sailed to Troy to wage war against the city in an attempt to return Helen to her husband, Menelaus. That was a thinly veiled reason, though. It was clear that Agamemnon wanted to wage the war for the sake of victory. He was one of the earliest examples of a straight-up warmonger. You may remember him from the 2004 movie *Troy*, which shows a pretty accurate representation of Agamemnon's personality (there was little to redeem him).

The Story You Need to Know

Much of Agamemnon's story comes from the *Iliad*, the story of the Trojan War and one of the oldest works of literature (see the entry on Clytemnestra and Her Children for the gory end to his story).

Many years into the Trojan War (it lasted ten in all), the Greeks' number one hero, Achilles, was fed up with how Agamemnon was handling things. The Greeks had raided and plundered many nearby cities and towns. One of the women they captured as a slave was named Chryseis, and her father, a priest of Apollo, had come to the Greeks, pleading for them to release her. Agamemnon refused, and so Apollo caused a plague to descend upon the Greeks as payback. When the plague got bad enough, Agamemnon finally gave in and returned Chryseis to her father (it had to get *really bad* before he agreed to it). But there was a caveat: He would give up Chryseis, a woman he'd taken possession of (awful), but in return, he would take Briseis, a woman Achilles had taken possession of (also awful). This decision caused Achilles to vow not to help the Greeks any further with their war against the Trojans. Neither he nor his men, the Myrmidons, partook in any further battles.

At first, Agamemnon kept up a brave face, but it quickly became very clear that the Greeks *really needed Achilles*. Achilles was the most powerful warrior, a son of a goddess. Agamemnon and the other Greeks tried for as long as they could to survive against the Trojans without him, but the Trojans had Hector, another skilled warrior, and the Greeks were no match for him without Achilles.

Throughout the war, the gods interfered in the fates of the Greeks and the Trojans. Athena and Hera did all they could to help the Greeks win, their hatred of Troy in part based on Paris's decision to side with Aphrodite in the Judgment of Paris. Meanwhile, Apollo, Aphrodite, and sometimes Zeus helped the Trojans in their attempts to defeat the Greeks.

Eventually, Agamemnon realized they had to get Achilles back on their side. With some of the other Greek leaders, he came up with the most generous collection of offerings he could think of in an effort to entice Achilles. They offered Achilles everything he could possibly want, but nothing could convince him to let go of his pride and rejoin the Greeks in their war against the Trojans (see the entry on Achilles and Patroclus for what it took to get him back).

Now You Know

A golden funeral mask known as the Mask of Agamemnon was found at the ancient Bronze Age site of Mycenae. It probably didn't actually belong to Agamemnon, but the man who found it *really* wanted to believe the Trojan War was real so he named it that. More, similar funeral masks were found that suggest the one named for Agamemnon was just one of many.

ACHILLES and PATROCLUS

A Prince of Phthia and His Longtime Companion

ᔕᘓᔕᘓᔕᘓᔕᘓ

What's Their Deal?

Achilles was the son of Peleus, the king of Phthia, and Thetis, the daughter of the sea god Nereus, a goddess and nymph of the sea. It was at Achilles's parents' wedding that the Apple of Discord caused such a momentous argument between goddesses. Patroclus had traveled to Phthia as a boy. He had killed another child accidentally and sought purification in Phthia (this was how murder was handled—you traveled to another city and asked their leader for purification). There, Achilles and Patroclus grew up together and became very close.

You may know Achilles and Patroclus from Madeline Miller's novel *The Song of Achilles*, in which their relationship is expanded into a romance, or from the 2004 film *Troy*, in which Achilles is played by Brad Pitt and the pair are instead depicted as cousins (while their romantic status is debated, they were *definitely* not cousins).

The Story You Need to Know

Achilles and Patroclus's story comes almost exclusively from Homer's *Iliad*, just like many of the other heroes of the Trojan War. Their tale revolved around the actions of Agamemnon and the sheer stubbornness of Achilles. Before Achilles officially withdrew himself and the Myrmidons from the war with Troy, he spoke with his mother, the goddess Thetis. He told her what Agamemnon had done, stealing the woman who Achilles had already stolen for himself, and Thetis in turn pleaded with Zeus to help Achilles by punishing the Greeks, allowing the Trojans to push them to the brink.

Even when Agamemnon was so desperate as to offer Achilles every gift he or the other Greeks could imagine, Achilles refused to return to the war. He felt so slighted that giving in and helping the Greeks would only embarrass him further. Achilles could not bear to feel as though he weren't the most important and righteous person in the group. But everything changed when Nestor (one of the Argonauts) asked Patroclus to help the Greeks. Most of their important leaders had been wounded, and things were looking pretty bad. Nestor encouraged Patroclus to take Achilles's armor and disguise himself as the hero. He told Patroclus that it would only serve to scare the Trojans and that Patroclus would be safe with the other Greeks. He just needed to look like Achilles, not be him.

Patroclus was moved by Nestor's speech. He was sad to see all the Greeks dying and injured, and Patroclus was not as stubborn as Achilles. So, at Nestor's suggestion, Patroclus tried to convince Achilles to lend him his armor. He reassured Achilles that he wouldn't be hurt and that he'd have the other Greeks to protect him—he just needed to appear as though he were Achilles. Achilles agreed, and Patroclus put the armor on and rode out to battle as though he were the hero himself.

Tragically, though, things didn't go as planned. Hector was there, and he went after the man he believed to be Achilles. Hector killed Patroclus. This was the push Achilles needed—he was horrified and heartbroken. Once he'd mourned Patroclus, all he wanted to do was kill Hector. Achilles went absolutely crazy on the battlefield, killing everyone in his path including, eventually, Hector himself.

The grief Achilles experienced at the death of Patroclus is one of the most memorable moments of the *Iliad*. It serves to redeem the character of Achilles, who had, up to that point, been incredibly frustrating and entitled.

The *Iliad* ends shortly after the death of Hector, but Achilles met his end closer to the end of the war, when he was shot through the ankle by one of Paris's arrows. His ankle was said to be his one vulnerable spot. As a child, his mother had dipped him in a potion of immortality, but there was one place the potion never reached: his Achilles heel.

Now You Know

It's not explicitly said that Achilles and Patroclus were in a romantic relationship, but there is a lot of evidence for it. The two were inseparable and loved each other dearly. It's been theorized that they were in fact longtime romantic partners, a theory that is built on in Miller's beautiful novel.

CLYTEMNESTRA
AND HER CHILDREN

Wife of Agamemnon; Queen of Mycenae;
and Her Children, Iphigenia, Orestes, and Electra

What's Their Deal?

Clytemnestra was the sister of Helen, daughter of Zeus and Leda, a princess of Sparta before she married Agamemnon (the brother of Helen's first husband, Menelaus), and queen of Mycenae. Clytemnestra and Agamemnon had three children, Iphigenia, Orestes, and Electra (in some accounts, there is a fourth, a daughter, Chrysothemis).

Iphigenia died young, because she was sacrificed by her father, Agamemnon. Agamemnon was the leader of the Greeks as they planned to wage war against Troy for the actions of Paris and Helen, but he had angered the goddess Artemis, and because of that, there were no winds at all as the fleet prepared to leave the port of Aulis. Agamemnon was told that sacrificing his daughter would solve this problem, so he told Iphigenia that she was to be given in marriage to the famous, beautiful prince Achilles, and he brought her to what she believed would be the ceremony. There he killed her. This decision would be his ruin (and rightly so).

The Story You Need to Know

Agamemnon returned from the Trojan War after ten years away from his home and his family in Mycenae. He returned not alone, but with a woman he brought back to be his slave, Cassandra. Cassandra was a princess of Troy and a powerful prophetess who was cursed never to be believed. While Agamemnon was away, though, Clytemnestra had been plotting with his archenemy, Aegisthus. Aegisthus was Agamemnon's cousin, and he had tried to gain control of Mycenae and had been locked up for it. Clytemnestra freed him, however, and they developed a relationship in Agamemnon's absence. The pair plotted and planned and were ready when the king returned from war. As soon as Agamemnon entered the palace, Clytemnestra led him to a bath she had drawn for him. Once he was in the bath, she and Aegisthus brutally murdered Agamemnon. It was, quite literally, a bloodbath.

Clytemnestra and Agamemnon's remaining children, Orestes and Electra, were not on the side of their mother in this decision, and they wanted to avenge their father's murder. While Agamemnon was at war, Orestes had been sent away and only returned upon his father's death. He revealed himself to his sister, and she shared her fury at their mother for her actions. Together, the pair planned and carried out the murder of their mother, Clytemnestra, and her lover, Aegisthus. Some sources say that Orestes carried it out, while others say it was Electra.

After the murder, Orestes was pursued by the Erinyes (the Furies) as punishment. Eventually, he was able to perform the necessary rites to purify himself, and the Erinyes finally left him alone.

Now You Know

While much of this story has roots in Homer (the fate of Agamemnon is mentioned in the *Odyssey*), the details come from a series of tragedies that were written and performed on the subject. All three major tragedians (those whose work survived the more than 2,400 years) wrote plays about this story: Aeschylus, Sophocles, and Euripides.

Aeschylus's *Oresteia* is the only surviving trilogy in Greek tragedy. It is composed of three plays covering Agamemnon's return and death (*Agamemnon*), Orestes's return and the murder of Clytemnestra and Aegisthus (*The Libation Bearers*), and the punishment of Orestes by trial and the Erinyes (*The Eumenides*). Sophocles wrote *Electra* about the murder of Clytemnestra, and Euripides wrote *Electra* and *Orestes* about the murder and the aftermath.

The Eumenides means "the kindly ones" and referred to the Erinyes, the Furies, whose role was to punish murderers, specifically murderers of family members. They were called that out of fear of angering them further by using their true name.

ODYSSEUS

King of Ithaca

AKA: Ulysses (Roman/Latin)

⌐⌐⌐⌐⌐⌐⌐

What's His Deal?

Odysseus was the ruler of the city Ithaca and the hero of Homer's *Odyssey*. The *Odyssey* tells the story of Odysseus after the end of the Trojan War and details his gaffe- and tragedy-filled journey home to Ithaca (see the entries on Paris, Achilles and Patroclus, and Agamemnon for more on the Trojan War and the *Iliad*).

Odysseus is best known for his wiliness and cunning. He was a trickster if there ever was one. Throughout the *Iliad* (and therefore throughout the Trojan War), Odysseus was known for being one of the few level-headed Greeks. You may know him from the 2004 movie *Troy*, in which he was played by Sean Bean. The *Odyssey* has also been adapted and retold countless times, such as in James Joyce's famous novel *Ulysses* and the 2000 movie *O Brother, Where Art Thou?*

Odysseus didn't want to be in Troy (he'd gone to great lengths to avoid the war, but to no avail), but if he had to be there he would at least try to be reasonable. Odysseus was married to Penelope, a princess of Sparta and cousin of Helen and Clytemnestra. Just before the war started, Odysseus and Penelope had a son named Telemachus. Before Telemachus could even walk, though, Odysseus sailed off to war with Troy and didn't come back for *twenty years.*

The Story You Need to Know

Many years after the end of the Trojan War, Odysseus was stranded on the island of the nymph Calypso. He had started out with a bunch of ships and many men as they sailed the Mediterranean back to Greece, but now none were left. Calypso wanted to marry Odysseus. He'd been there for seven years, but at that point he just wanted to get home to his wife and son (sure, he'd had some fun with Calypso over those years; he's no saint…but he was ready to go home). When he was finally free of Calypso's island (on orders from the gods), he ended up on the island of the Phaeacians. There, he told them his story:

First, he told them, he and his men landed on the island of the Lotus-Eaters. Odysseus quickly learned they were in trouble there, because the Lotus-Eaters offered his men lotus to eat, which immediately rid them of their memories and their desire to return to Ithaca. Next, they landed on the island of the Cyclopes, where a number of Odysseus's men were eaten. They fled that island as quickly as they could and ended up next on the island of Aeolus, a divine entity who controlled the winds. Aeolus gifted Odysseus with a bag containing the West Wind and instructed him how to get back to Ithaca. The crew sailed day and night, and, finally, when Ithaca was in sight, Odysseus allowed himself to take a nap. But his men were curious about what Aeolus had given as a gift, and they opened the bag. In so doing, they let out the West Wind, which blew the ships so far off course they were once again lost in the middle of the Mediterranean Sea. Odysseus was not thrilled.

After the wind incident, Odysseus and his men landed on the island of the Laestrygonians, a race of people who they quickly learned were cannibals. They rushed to leave the island, but many of the ships were trapped in the island's harbor and weren't able to escape. *Many* of Odysseus's men died on that island.

Finally, what remained of the ships landed on yet another island, this one called Aiaia and ruled by a woman, a witch named Circe. Circe told Odysseus that in order to continue on, he'd need to visit the Underworld itself. He did, speaking with the dead and learning what he'd need to do to finally get to Ithaca. Once that was done, Odysseus and his remaining men had strict instructions from Circe on how to avoid the next hurdles they'd face. First were the Sirens—the men must avoid hearing the song of these monstrous women in order to pass by. Next, they would encounter the deadly sea monsters Scylla and Charybdis. Finally, they would stop on the island of Thrinacia. On Thrinacia, they were told explicitly not to eat the sacred cows of Helios that grazed there. But Odysseus's men didn't listen, and this was how Odysseus ended up all alone on Calypso's island (*every one* of his men had died).

Meanwhile, in Ithaca, Penelope had been fighting off suitors all those years! She and Telemachus were biding their time, hoping maybe Odysseus would come back, but mostly just hating the suitors and everything they'd done over the many, many years. They were eating them out of house and home in addition to being just plain obnoxious. Finally, with the help of the Phaeacians, who gave Odysseus a ride, he arrived in Ithaca. But before he let anyone know he was there, he plotted what to do next. Eventually he returned to his palace, disguised as a beggar. During a nighttime feast, he and his now twenty-year-old son, Telemachus, killed every one of the suitors who had been troubling Penelope all those years (over one hundred of them!) before Odysseus finally revealed himself to his wife. He was home safe after twenty years.

Now You Know

When Odysseus was trying to avoid going to war against Troy, he pretended to have lost his mind so he wouldn't have to go. The Greeks arrived in Ithaca to bring Odysseus to war, and to prove he'd lost it, Odysseus sowed his own fields with salt instead of seeds. But the Greeks suspected he was tricking them, so they placed Odysseus's baby son in front of him as he sowed, knowing he wouldn't risk harming his son. They were right, and when Telemachus was at risk, Odysseus gave up the game and went away with them to war.

Polyphemus

A Cyclopes

———————◆◆◆———————

Polyphemus was a Cyclopes, a one-eyed giant. While the original three Cyclopes were the children of Gaia and Ouranos and therefore some of the oldest creatures of Greek mythology, Polyphemus was a younger Cyclopes, instead a child of the god Poseidon and the nymph Thoosa. As the son of Poseidon, Polyphemus was beloved by the god (this is important).

Polyphemus had an island to himself, and across a narrow stretch of sea lay another island where more Cyclopes lived. But Polyphemus lived on his own with flocks of sheep and goats as his only companions. He was alone until, one day, the ships of Odysseus landed on his island, and Odysseus and his men arrived, wandering in search of food or inhabitants. Polyphemus was out at his pastures with his animals when the men came upon the cave where he lived and stored his food and some animals. Odysseus and his men gorged themselves on Polyphemus's food, not knowing who or what lived in the cave (a risky move!). Finally, Polyphemus returned home and shut up the cave with an enormous boulder that only he, a giant, could move. Odysseus and his men hid in the cave, watching for what Polyphemus would do next. Polyphemus, when he saw the men, asked what they were doing there before changing speeds: He picked up a number of Odysseus's men and smashed them together before ripping them limb from limb while the rest stood by watching.

That night, they tried to sleep. Polyphemus had a full stomach, having eaten Odysseus's men and quite a lot of cheese. He lay back and went to sleep, not worried about the remaining men trapped in his cave. Odysseus, meanwhile, realized he could never move the boulder blocking the cave himself; he needed Polyphemus to do that. The next day, Odysseus and what remained of his men (Polyphemus had eaten a few more for breakfast) were left alone to plot and plan, still trapped in the cave, while Polyphemus did his daily tasks in the field. When Polyphemus returned, Odysseus offered him wine, and then more wine. Odysseus got Polyphemus drunk and they chatted. Odysseus tried to be friendly with the Cyclopes and explained that his name was Nobody.

Before long, Polyphemus was drunk enough that he fell asleep, and Odysseus took the opportunity to stab him in his one eye, blinding him. Polyphemus cried out in pain, "Nobody has blinded me!" When the Cyclopes on the adjacent island heard this, they were confused and offered no help. Finally, in his anguish, Polyphemus removed the boulder from the doorway to the cave and attempted to stand guard, even in his blinded state, so that Odysseus and his men couldn't escape. But the men were crafty and managed to attach themselves to the undersides of Polyphemus's sheep. The sheep made their way out of the cave and down to their pasture. Polyphemus felt the tops of the sheep as they were leaving and, feeling their woolly coats, let them pass. When Odysseus and his men, still attached to the sheep, were far enough from Polyphemus's cave, they freed themselves and fled to their ships, with Polyphemus crying out after them. As he was sailing off, Odysseus called back, revealing to Polyphemus that his name was in fact Odysseus of Ithaca. With this information, Polyphemus told his father, Poseidon, what had been done to him, and Poseidon vowed to make ruin of Odysseus and his ships (this plan was very successful, as evidenced in Odysseus's entry).

Circe

A Goddess of Sorcery and Magic

AKA: Kirke (alternate spelling)

———◆———

Circe was a goddess of magic, herself a witch. You may know her from the Madeline Miller novel named for her, *Circe*. She was the daughter of the Titan Helios and the nymph Perseis; the sister of Aeëtes and Pasiphaë (yes, the same Pasiphaë); and, through her brother Aeëtes, aunt of yet another witch, Medea. Circe lived on the mysterious island of Aiaia with nymphs as companions and lions and wolves as her pets.

When Odysseus and his men landed on Circe's island, she sought to defend herself against the strange men who had arrived without warning. A group of the men went in search of the island's inhabitants and came across Circe's palace. She made a show of welcoming them inside and offering them food and drink. But once they were full, she used her magic and transformed them all into pigs, which she shut away in a pen. She then

went about her life on the island—not realizing that one of the men had stayed outside her palace and witnessed it all.

Eurylochus, the man who escaped Circe, ran back to Odysseus and the men and told them what had happened at the witch's palace. Hearing this, Odysseus and the men (except Eurylochus—he was too scared and stayed by the ships) went to the palace to free the men from Circe. En route, however, Odysseus was stopped by the god Hermes, who told him how to avoid Circe's magic and gave him an herb that would prevent it from being used on him. When the men arrived at the palace, Circe welcomed them just as she had before. She gave the men food and drink and then moved to transform them just as she had their shipmates. Much to Circe's surprise and annoyance, her magic didn't work on Odysseus! Instead, he came at her with his sword, and she fell to her knees, knowing immediately who he was: She'd been told by the same god who helped Odysseus, Hermes, that a brave man by that name would come to her island on his way from Troy.

She suggested he ditch his sword and go to bed with her. Convinced she was going to free his men eventually, Odysseus agreed (he'd been away from home so long!). After they slept together and Odysseus had a nice, relaxing bath, Circe did indeed transform Odysseus's men back into men and let them live freely on her island. Odysseus and his men stayed there for some time, with Odysseus developing a relationship with Circe before she helped them continue on their journey home to Ithaca.

Scylla and Charybdis

Two Deadly Monsters

———◆———

Scylla and Charybdis were a pair of monsters that primarily feature in Homer's *Odyssey*. They worked together to kill anyone who tried to sail between them. Scylla was a monstrous creature with dangling legs and six snakelike necks with snarling, frothing heads that featured razor-sharp teeth, and from the mouths echoed a booming, doglike bark. She lived atop a cliffside on one side of a narrow strait. On the other side of the strait was Charybdis, a sentient and violent whirlpool that would suck ships into her depths with incredible force. The strait where Scylla and Charybdis terrorized sailors was believed to be the Strait of Messina, between Sicily and the Italian mainland.

One of the last obstacles faced by Odysseus and his men as they attempted to return home to Ithaca after the Trojan War was to sail through this strait guarded by Scylla and Charybdis. The men received instruction from Circe on how best to make it through the treacherous strait: Sail closer to Scylla, and know that some will die; otherwise Charybdis would take the whole ship into her depths. Odysseus followed the instructions, and as expected, Scylla was able to use her many heads to pull men from the deck before devouring them in full view of their shipmates below. Still, as they passed, they watched Charybdis suck all the water around her in the swirl of the whirlpool so deep that they could see the sea floor in the center!

But that was only the first time Odysseus passed through the strait. After Odysseus's men mistakenly ate the cows of Helios, Odysseus alone had to sail back through the strait. That time he wasn't able to avoid Charybdis, and instead he leapt off his ship to grab hold of a fig tree just as Charybdis sucked the ship into the depths. Odysseus hung on precariously to the tree, waiting for whatever was left of his ship to be spewed back out. Finally, his mast shot out from the whirlpool of Charybdis, and Odysseus grabbed on to it. Hanging on to the mast, Odysseus floated until he reached the island of the nymph Calypso.

FURTHER READING (AND LISTENING)!

There are *lots* of books and podcasts out there if you want to learn more about Greek (and/or Roman) mythology. Here's a short list of some of my favorites as suggestions.

More About Mythology

These are deeper dives into the mythology (and history) of ancient Greece and beyond, from modern-ish writers and historians.

⋘ *Mythology: Timeless Tales of Gods and Heroes* by Edith Hamilton (timeless indeed!)

⋘ *The Greek Myths* by Robert Graves (extensive!)

⋘ *Mythos* and *Heroes* by Stephen Fry

⋘ *The Amazons* by Adrienne Mayor (fascinating!)

⋘ *The Marriage of Cadmus and Harmony* by Roberto Calasso (not quite original mythology, not quite fiction, but it's *so* beautiful)

⋘ *Let's Talk About Myths, Baby! A Greek and Roman Mythology Podcast* by Liv Albert (a little self-promotion…a casual and very detailed podcast retelling Greek and Roman myths)

The Mythology Itself!

These are primary sources, works written in the ancient world about the mythology and what the ancient Greeks (and Romans, in two cases) believed.

- *The Golden Ass* by Apuleius (my favorite translation is by Sarah Ruden)

- Homer's *Iliad* and *Odyssey* (my favorite *Odyssey* translation is by Emily Wilson, and she's working on the *Iliad* too)

- *Homeric Hymns* (fascinating, and about as old as Homer!)

- *Metamorphoses* and *Heroides* by Ovid (a Roman poet who retold what were mostly originally Greek myths in visceral, and often sympathetic, detail)

- Any plays by Euripides, Sophocles, Aeschylus, or Aristophanes (standouts include Euripides's *Medea*, *The Bacchae*, and *Electra*; Aeschylus's *Oresteia* trilogy; Sophocles's *Oedipus Tyrannos* [sometimes called *Oedipus Rex*]; and Aristophanes's *Lysistrata* and *The Frogs*)

Fiction Based in Mythology

Modern fiction based on, or retelling, mythology of the ancient Greeks.

- *The Penelopiad* by Margaret Atwood (a retelling of the *Odyssey* through the eyes of Penelope)

- *The Silence of the Girls* by Pat Barker (the *Iliad* and the Trojan War through the lens of the women of Troy)

- *The Children of Jocasta* by Natalie Haynes (a gorgeous retelling of the story of Oedipus, Jocasta, and their children)

- *A Thousand Ships* by Natalie Haynes (the stories of Homer's epics from the perspective of the women involved)

- *Circe* by Madeline Miller (the life story of the witch goddess Circe)

- *The Song of Achilles* by Madeline Miller (a *stunning* retelling of the romance between Achilles and Patroclus, their lives, and the Trojan War)

- *Lore Olympus* by Rachel Smythe (a beautiful Webtoon with a modern take on myths, mainly Persephone and Hades)

- *House of Names* by Colm Tóibín (a retelling of the story of Clytemnestra and her children)

INDEX

Note: Page numbers in **bold** indicate primary entries of characters.

ABOUT THE AUTHOR

Liv Albert is obsessed with Greek mythology. She has a degree in classical civilizations and English literature from Concordia University in Montreal and a postgraduate certificate in creative book publishing from Humber College in Toronto. In a past life she worked on other people's books, negotiating contracts for a major publisher in Toronto. Liv started the *Let's Talk About Myths, Baby!* podcast in 2017, growing it from the ramblings of a woman in her living room to the ramblings of a woman in her *den*, where it is now one of the biggest independent podcasts in Canada with millions of downloads per year. She lives in Victoria, BC, Canada, in a mythology-filled apartment with her cat, Lupin.

ABOUT THE ILLUSTRATOR

Sara Richard is an Eisner and Ringo Award–nominated artist from New Hampshire. She has worked in the comic book industry for eight years, mainly as a cover artist. Before that, she was a toy sculptor at Hasbro, specializing in making tiny dinosaurs. Sara's inspiration comes from Art Deco, Art Nouveau, 1980s fashion, and Victorian-era design. When not making art or writing, she's watching horror movies, cleaning forgotten gravestones, and collecting possibly haunted curios from the nineteenth century. Her online gallery can be found at SaraRichard.com.